Krav Maga for Women

Krav Maga for Women

Your Ultimate Program for Self-Defense

DARREN LEVINE
RYAN HOOVER
KELLY CAMPBELL

Photographs by Dominic DiSaia

 Ulysses Press

In memory of Marni

———

Published in the United States by
ULYSSES PRESS
P.O. Box 3440
Berkeley, CA 94703
www.ulyssespress.com

ISBN: 978-1-56975-987-5
Library of Congress Control Number 2011926030

Printed in Canada by Webcom

10 9 8 7 6 5 4 3 2 1

Contributing writer	Margot Cotter
Acquisitions	Keith Riegert
Editorial/Production	Lily Chou, Claire Chun, Lauren Harrison, Judith Metzener
Index	Sayre Van Young
Design	what!design @ whatweb.com
Photographs	Dominic DiSaia except on pages 38 and 39 © Paul Reavlin
Models	Tina Angelotti, Jarrett Arthur, Kelly Campbell, Jon Catoe, Naama Chezar, Jeff Fredericksen, Ryan Hoover, Darren Levine, Jacqueline Jimenez Maldonado, Tamara Podemski, Matthew Romond, Rafael Malpica Uscanga

Visit Krav Maga Worldwide online at www.kravmaga.com

Distributed by Publishers Group West

Please Note
This book has been written and published strictly for informational purposes, and in no way should be used as a substitute for actual instruction with qualified professionals. The author and publisher are providing you with information in this work so that you can have the knowledge and can choose, at your own risk, to act on that knowledge. The author and publisher also urge all readers to be aware of their health status and to consult health care professionals before beginning any health program.

Table of Contents

Why Krav Maga for Women?   5

What Is Krav Maga?   7

Training Methodology   11

Use of Force: How Much Force Can I Use to Defend Myself?   15

Surviving the Encounter   20

What to Do If You're Raped or Assaulted   32

TECHNIQUES

Getting Started   37

Striking Basics   40

    Straight Punches   45

    Hammerfist Punches   49

    Elbow Strikes   53

    Kicks   63

    Kicks from a Lying Position   77

Defenses against Unarmed Attacks   83

    Defense against Wrist and Arm Pulls   111

    Defense against Bearhugs   134

Groundfighting   150

Using Everyday Objects as Defensive Weapons   166

Dealing with Multiple Attackers   174

Defenses against Handgun Threats   178

Defenses against Edged-Weapon Threats   192

    Edged-Weapon Threats from the Front   194

    Edged-Weapon Threats from Behind   197

Index   200

Acknowledgments   203

About the Authors   204

Why Krav Maga for Women?

Krav Maga for Women is about teaching women how to protect themselves against violent attacks that may occur in almost any modern-day scenario. The lessons in this book apply to attacks against you and threats to your safety during a street crime, common battery, robbery, carjacking, etc. Additionally, we address crimes related to sexual assaults, which are at epidemic proportions in the United States.

The book contains important life-saving Krav Maga techniques adopted especially for the needs of women. This book will also serve to increase awareness, build sound tactical reasoning in order to avoid danger, and, should the need arise, present the finest, most realistic methods for women to defend themselves in a time of need.

Why Krav Maga for women? This question, admittedly, is one that Krav Maga Worldwide considered when beginning this book project, since the Krav Maga mantra "it's designed for everyone" is fundamental to our philosophy. So, why did we feel a book focusing on women was necessary?

While the Krav Maga defensive techniques certainly are designed for everyone, it'd be short-sighted to ignore the physical and social differences of men and women. In truth, women generally have less upper body strength than men do. Men have traditionally been involved in more competitive sports, particularly those involving contact. Women during their youth are not typically subjected to the same level of schoolyard scuffles as male classmates. Historically, the tenets of society engender us to frown upon girls engaging in activities that are typically reserved for boys. In social settings as adults, men are more likely to be involved in ego-driven confrontations, while women are more likely to be the subjects of verbal or physical assaults of a more sexual nature. There are certainly other examples that can further illustrate the differences between men and women, but this begins to explain our motivation for creating a book designed especially for the needs of women.

The most important point relative to this book is that women serve in the Israeli military, and have done so in some shape or form since the inception of the nation. Israel, in terms of its geographical region was, and currently is, greatly outnumbered by other military forces in the Middle East. The Israel Defense Forces (IDF) had to be supported by a wider range of the population compared to most Western forces. For example, men serve in the IDF well into their fifties and, as mentioned earlier, women also put in their time. Krav Maga emerged in an environment where there was extreme violence, mostly related to the threat of terrorism, and the strong likelihood of war with neighbors was of the highest concern.

The total integration of women and older men in the Israeli military necessitated that a hand-to-hand combat and self-defense system be developed that would be effective for all who serve. Krav Maga is the system taught to Israeli women to prepare them to serve in combat. In fact, Krav Maga is a critical part of the combat-readiness training for women who serve in the IDF as well as the National Police Force, the Israeli Secret Service, and the Israeli Intelligence Service. For women, there is no self-defense system in the world more street and battle tested than Krav Maga.

If you're familiar with Krav Maga training, you likely won't notice significant differences in the techniques in this book, but you may note shifts in technical or tactical emphasis in some of the techniques or situations. While you may never be able to completely prevent yourself from being sexually assaulted, there are some things you can do to defend yourself against an attacker and to help reduce your risk of being assaulted.

What Is Krav Maga?

Krav Maga was originally developed in Israel as the official system of self-defense and hand-to-hand combat for the Israel Defense Forces (IDF), the Israeli National Police, Israeli Special Operations, and other security units. More recently, Krav Maga has been taught extensively to civilians, law-enforcement agencies, and military units in the United States and to our allies throughout the world.

Cognizant of the different use-of-force standards between Israel and the United States, Krav Maga Worldwide took important steps to refine and adapt Krav Maga techniques for use by American law enforcement and civilians.

The System

Krav Maga has a worldwide reputation as being an ideal means of defending one's life or the life of a third party, whether the threat involves unarmed assailants, armed assailants, or multiple assailants. The Krav Maga Worldwide system has received exceptional international recognition as the leading modern-day innovative and highly practical self-defense system ideally suited for three distinct entities: law enforcement, military, and civilians.

Krav Maga is a no-nonsense, no-frills system that is designed to instill a fighting spirit and aggressive mindset in its students. Techniques, in a vacuum, are useless. Without developing aggressiveness or fighting spirit, the techniques will not matter because under duress the defender will be unable to react in a timely or effective manner. The student/defender must train in a way that will promote and enhance decisive action under extreme stress and/or fatigue.

While Krav Maga recognizes that self-defense is not punishment and that the ultimate goal is to go home safely, the tenets dictate that the best way to achieve that goal is to react aggressively and decisively. For women, this is even more important, since women generally have less muscle mass to cushion or absorb blows and are not as accustomed to the type of hard contact that comes with a violent encounter.

Perhaps the most important characteristics of the system are:

Practical Techniques   The main emphasis of the Krav Maga system is on effectiveness, simplicity, and sound, logical problem solving. This is a street-fighting system that provides realistic defenses against a variety of aggressive attacks, whether the assailant is armed or unarmed, and whether the attack is directed at you or a third party. The system is well integrated, which means techniques and principles that are taught will be applicable in more than one situation, allowing students to learn select principles dealing with reaction time, defense, and counterattacks that will apply to a multitude of different attacks.

Don't Get Hurt   While this may seem obvious, the intent is far-reaching. This principle dictates that great lengths should be taken to avoid conflict if at all possible. Often, an improved understanding of the dynamics of violence and violent people will heighten awareness and avoidance. This "hypervigilance" may be even more important for women, since avoiding a violent encounter is the best way to ensure "success." However, if avoidance is not possible, it's imperative that the defender be aggressive in order to eliminate the threat as quickly as possible, thus diminishing the chances for injury.

Efficient Training Period   Students attain a high level of proficiency in a relatively short period of instruction. Krav Maga training today has been further refined to meet the needs of citizens and law-enforcement personnel tasked with other priorities, missions, endeavors, and responsibilities in daily life. Krav Maga Worldwide's training methodology is specifically designed to build a warrior using uniquely minimal training time. The system also allows students to achieve life-saving skills in a relatively short period of time.

Training from Positions of Disadvantage   Life, by its very nature, makes even the most vigilant trainee prone to distraction. Whether it's a mental lapse, complacency, or, worse, apathy, lapses are natural. Krav Maga training takes such realities into consideration and forces students to train from a poor state of readiness. Understanding that it's highly probable that a defender will be forced to take action when unprepared, training is typically conducted from a neutral position. This position forces the student to perform techniques without regard to proper footwork, hand positioning, balance, weight distribution, etc. In order for training to be the most effective for reality, the techniques and tactics must not rely on being prepared.

Retention of Training   The Krav Maga system is based on common principles and natural, instinctive reactions to danger. This means Krav Maga techniques can be retained with minimal review and practice.

Performing Techniques Under Stress and Other Conditions That Replicate Reality   Unique training methods are a key ingredient to the Krav Maga system and are specifically designed to replicate the realities that exist in a life-threatening encounter. The training is designed to improve one's emotional and physical response to danger and is used to develop the ability to recognize danger at its earliest stages, to go from absolutely no, or a low, state of readiness to a state of action without hesitation, to develop a warrior's mindset, to engage and overcome an adversary, and to escalate and de-escalate using appropriate levels of force.

Addressing Immediate Dangers First   Without addressing the true problem, no "technique" can be successful. Krav Maga stresses that the most imminent danger must be taken care of first, and that it should be done in the most efficient fashion. In the moment an attack happens, this approach is all that matters and not only serves to address the immediate danger, but, if done effectively, subsequent dangers.

Using What Your Body Does Naturally   While other styles or systems may teach techniques that some may deem "better" under given circumstances, most often these techniques work against the body's natural reactions and require extensive time in training. Techniques such as these are less likely to work under the stress of a violent encounter. Many of these techniques also require the defender to be as strong if not stronger than the attacker. Since weight classes aren't part of sexual assaults, this approach is definitely not ideal for giving women the best chance of success.

Krav Maga techniques are gross motor by design. In other words, the techniques use big movements driven by the whole body, instead of relying on fine motor skills, which fail under stress. When possible, the techniques also draw heavily from what the body would most likely do naturally. This approach increases the likelihood of performing a technique successfully during the stress of a real-life violent encounter. It also lessens the amount of training time needed in order to be effective. For the average woman, and that is the focus, many hours per week "on the mat" is not practical.

Hitting Back Early and Often   A strong counterattack is vital to any realistic defense. A strong and aggressive counter is designed to disrupt the ongoing attack. It forces the attacker to react to the defender, as opposed to continuing or adjusting the attack. The sooner this attack is delivered, the quicker the defender is able to shift, at least emotionally, from "victim" to "victor." Remember, most criminals are looking for an easy target, not someone who fights back fiercely. Therefore, an aggressive and immediate counterattack will also serve to surprise the attacker, creating openings for further counters and escape. Defensive actions alone do not "win" an altercation. You must be trained and psychologically prepared to inflict damage on your attacker.

While violent attacks rarely occur in a controlled environment, it's more likely the case that women will be sexually assaulted in their homes, vehicles, and other places they regularly frequent. This may provide a strategic advantage for the defender, who can use her familiarity with the "lay of the land" to her advantage. It's still important to evaluate every environment to determine the common objects present to use to defend or attack, routes of escape, and other actions to ensure your survival. (See page 168 for more information about using common objects to your advantage.)

Where Can You Train in Krav Maga?

Krav Maga Worldwide, at the printing of this book, recognizes over 240 officially licensed training facilities worldwide. These training centers are required to have certified instructors teaching the Krav Maga classes, and the centers and instructors are held to very high training and teaching standards. The certification process is very demanding, with 30 to 40 percent of instructor candidates failing the initial phase of training. An up-to-date certified instructor is not only tasked with teaching techniques in a manner that can be assimilated quickly, but must devise and implement training methods and drills that allow students to gain confidence and pressure-test abilities (in a relatively safe environment). For an updated listing of these centers, please visit the locations page of the Krav Maga Worldwide website at **www.kravmaga.com**.

Attacking Targets That Are Most Vulnerable   Krav Maga emphasizes attacking vulnerable areas, such as the eyes, jaw, throat, liver, kidneys, groin, fingers, knees, shins, and insteps. Strikes to these areas allow defenders to do maximum damage with minimal effort and strength.

Using the Environment to Your Advantage...or at Least Recognizing When It's Not   While many violent attacks don't occur in a controlled environment, it's more likely the case in many sexual assaults that women are attacked in their homes. While this may pro-vide a strategic advantage for the defender, who knows the "lay of the land," it's still important to evaluate the area in order to choose the proper action. As an example, if defending in a heavily furnished living room, upper body strikes may be preferred over kicks.

Krav Maga training emphasizes the use of com-mon objects found on the scene, either offen-sively (e.g., blunt object for striking) or defensively (e.g., chair as a shield), in order to increase the chances of surviving an attack. This is extremely important since fights are rarely "fair." Since women are more likely to face an attacker who is larger and stronger, they're at a greater disadvantage from the very onset of the attack. Using objects found in the environment gives the defender the opportunity to end the encounter more quickly than otherwise possible or feasible.

Knowing That Quitting Isn't an Option   Proper Krav Maga training will go to great lengths, through specially designed drills, to develop a fighting spirit in each practitioner. In times of potential danger, many factors can affect the outcome of the altercation, and the attacker controls most of them, at least initially. That said, the fighting spirit developed through Krav Maga training may very well be the one factor under the defender's con-trol. Therefore, it must be nurtured and cultivated to become pervasive.

Krav Maga drills physically empower and, consequently, emotionally empower students. The systematic process of training under new and varied stressors serves to strengthen the skill set needed to perform in times of actual duress.

The essence of Krav Maga, and what will save the defender, is the willingness to do whatever it takes to sur-vive. The philosophy that a "never say die" attitude can be strengthened through training is the linchpin that allows Krav Maga students to adapt under the most stressful situations and emerge successfully from violent confrontations, regardless of the dynamic.

Getting Away   A "win" is not recognized by way of a hand being raised or a belt being worn. The goal is to go home safely—period. Krav Maga training stresses that it's critically important to defend aggressively to ensure that the threat is eliminated, but it's simultaneously important to avoid remaining in harm's way longer than is necessary. As time elapses, variables (introduction of weapons, additional attackers, fatigue, injury, etc.) increase. Therefore, the defender should look to leave the scene as soon as safely possible.

Use of Force Issues   Krav Maga Worldwide training enables people to defend themselves and deal with the most violent armed assailants, while remaining acutely aware of reasonable use of force and civil liabilities that arise during a violent encounter.

Training Methodology

In Krav Maga training sessions, the emphasis is on "replicating the reality of a brutal attack." By studying real-life violent encounters, we discover where victims fall prey to aggressors. What is it that occurs during a fight for one's life where people fail in their effort to react correctly to specific and non-specific dangers directed at them? The use of creative training methods to build the desired physiological and emotional response to danger is as vital as the physical techniques that exist in a defensive tactics system. What happens when an assailant really wants to hurt, torture, rape, and/or kill you? Has your training included operating under the stress of real-life conditions?

Students should be trained in a way that pushes limits, overwhelming them physically and emotionally. One must be forced to fight when attention is seriously challenged and divided, when vision is impaired, and when physical fatigue tries to persuade the mind and spirit to quit. Pushing students to these limits conditions them to control breathing, auditory and visual impairments, and the like while in a combative situation—to keep fighting even if shot, stabbed, or broken.

This section is not meant to be a tutorial on how to structure a Krav Maga class, nor will it address all of the training methods incorporated into Krav Maga Worldwide classes. The purpose of this section is to introduce and detail elements of training that should be a part of any good self-defense system.

Position of Disadvantage

As addressed in previous books, Krav Maga self-defense techniques are almost always trained from a neutral position or from a position of disadvantage. While it's certainly possible that a defender recognizes a threat early, training from a position of disadvantage (in the dark, with the emergence of an unknown threat or threats; while physically exhausted; with attention divided; having to make multiple tactical decisions in a correct sequence; functioning while injured or from a restricted position; etc.) is designed to inculcate in one a warrior spirit and skill set that help one to overcome physical, emotional, and spiritual obstacles, such as having to transition into action from a poor state of readiness. In other words, since students are often put into worst-case situations in their training sessions, performing in a true-life encounter where they're required to defend when more distracted, with a lower state of readiness, fear, etc., permits them to succeed because the training methods employed teach them to react and perform effectively under the conditions they'll face in real combat. They succeed because "you perform as you train" (or maybe even less) and the training drills have specifically prepared them to succeed under such dire circumstances.

Unfamiliar Surroundings

In addition to training from positions of disadvantage (in reference to the student's body), it's also important to train in unfamiliar and less-controlled surroundings. Always training on matted floors, with mirrors and with familiar points of reference, is not conducive to the most realistic training. Therefore, students should be exposed to training in areas such as parks, offices, parking garages/lots, vehicles, etc. The unfamiliar surroundings, in addition to varying terrains and obstacles, will broaden a student's understanding of the need for different solutions under different conditions. It's also fun!

Scenario Replication

Scenario replication is a vital part of Krav Maga Worldwide training. Simply changing environments or body postures, without situational scenarios, is not enough. In order for students to learn to critically analyze danger in an environment and gain situational awareness, they must apply Krav Maga principles appropriately. They should be put to the test by use of creative and relevant factual scenarios to enhance the training session. Situational drills will often determine appropriate pre-contact behavior, defensive techniques, tactics, use of force, etc. For example, a 35-year-old woman "placed" in an elevator with one seemingly inebriated and slightly agitated 60-year-old woman would likely undergo completely different adrenal, technical, and tactical responses than the same woman carrying her 10-month-old baby on an elevator with three belligerent and argumentative 20-year-olds. Without creative scenarios based on accurate accounts of real street crime, it's difficult for students to imagine circumstances that would force different physiological and tactical responses. Moreover, it's extremely difficult to react decisively under varying circumstances if training only consists of compliant or relatively compliant partners, in which the context is always the same or is never addressed.

Training Partners

It's extremely important to train with others and to train with as many different types of people as you can: short, tall, young, old, big, small, athletic, fast, strong, etc. A resisting "opponent" is invaluable to realistic self-defense training, and everyone has a different feel, energy, and approach. Being exposed to these differences is important to practical training.

Training Drills

Finally, training drills bring all of the other components together. Drills in Krav Maga classes account for anywhere from 10 to 30 percent of the allotted time, but training drills comprise as much as 50 percent of the total system. This is important to note since some other systems have great techniques and poor training drills, while others have poor techniques but great training drills. The Krav Maga Worldwide approach is to give equal or nearly equal relevance and attention to both.

How do professional football players prepare for game day? You may be surprised to learn that very little practice time is devoted to actually playing inter-squad games. Training consists of the use of thoughtful, creative, and carefully devised training drills that, in a concentrated format, improve skill sets and mentally prepare players for the stress of high-level, violent competition. Therefore, the effective use of drills must replicate the conditions present in a professional football game. In reality, the training session should bring the athletes to a point where performing in the game is easier than the high-level drills they must perform in preparation for a contest. Players must be pushed to their limits physically, emotionally, and spiritually in practice sessions, without being injured, so that these skills are available at game time. These practice sessions should produce the same chemical, physiological, and psychological responses that exist during an official and highly contested war-like game.

In dealing with deadly force scenarios, it's obvious that we cannot train under 100 percent realistic conditions. If we did, we would severely, even fatally, injure participants during the training sessions. So how can we prepare our students to survive violence—not only the physical attack but also the assault that is inflicted on all their senses and emotions? Trainers must build the mind-body component that ultimately controls whether or not one can respond with an effective physical technique to defeat an aggressor. You may be able to kick and punch in a controlled environment, but how do you respond when you're in tremendous fear, when you're fatigued, when your attention is divided, when you're injured but you must keep fighting? What good is it to learn effective techniques inside a controlled training room? It means nothing if you're not able to manage your body and mind and perform the defensive principles and techniques you've learned over hours, weeks, months, and years of training.

Every training drill must have at least a singular purpose to prepare the student for that which he or she will need in a street war. Every training drill must challenge the defender to perform under the most uncomfortable conditions, in which each one of the senses and emotions is tapped, tested, and severely challenged. Stress inoculation is a way to train people in preparation for battle. Students can be trained to avoid freezing during a violent encounter. They can be trained to see when tunnel vision is occurring. They can learn to "manage" physiological and emotional responses in order to operate at maximum capacity, while maintaining situational awareness. They can be trained to control breathing in order to reduce fatigue. They can be taught to overcome fear and turn fear into a positive force for survival.

While there are many benefits to training drills, some of the most important are:

- Improved reaction time
- Improved vision and awareness of the environment
- Controlling fatigue by breathing properly while under stress
- Ability to make correct tactical decisions while functioning under stress
- Enhanced critical thinking and physical performance
- Overcoming fear and confusion when being hit or disturbed
- Increased student confidence
- Better understanding of techniques, principles, and goals
- Improved class morale
- Improved fitness level using a combat-functional process
- Increased class energy

There are many genres of drills that can be employed to achieve these goals. For the purposes of this book, we'll highlight four:

Aggressiveness Drills   Designed to develop or enhance fighting spirit in students, such drills often require students to get through some sort of barrier or obstacle before, after, or while performing combatives or self-defense.

Fatigue Drills   Designed to push students to and just beyond a feeling of exhaustion and motivate them to do even more, fatigue drills typically involve a lot of aerobic and/or anaerobic movements devised to exhaust specific body parts or the entire body.

Awareness Drills   Designed to increase students' ability to recognize and/or track current threats or impending threats, these drills often require students to identify a target or threat and respond with the appropriate combative or tactical reaction, often while performing other tasks.

Stress Drills   Designed to develop or enhance the ability to perform under varying levels or types of stress, such drills typically require students to perform more than one task at a time, switch from one activity to another quickly, respond under extreme duress and/or uncomfortable circumstances, and may combine elements of other drill types.

Use of Force: How Much Force Can I Use to Defend Myself?

"Use of Force" law has applications in both in civil and criminal contexts. Established principles give civilians the right to apply force to the person of another and to engage in violence for the sole purpose of defending one's own life or the life of a third party from physical harm, great bodily injury, and/or even death.

What Is Force?

Force is any verbal or physical action taken to control, restrain, or stop another. If you make physical contact with another person in order to stop, disable, injure, or inflict great bodily injury, or even to kill them, your actions will be reviewed to determine if you acted as a "reasonable person" (see below for definition). In the context of this book, we address force used to keep you free from physical and emotional harm, serious bodily injury, or death. Generally, a person may lawfully react in self-defense, but only if she uses an amount of force that is reasonable to maintain her safety.

What Is the "Reasonable Person" Standard?

The legal phrase "reasonable person" describes a hypothetical person in the community who exercises average care, skill, and judgment in conduct. The determination of whether the defender is guilty involves the application of an objective test that compares your conduct to that of a reasonable person under the same or similar circumstances. Persons with greater than average skills, or with special duties to society, are usually held to a higher standard of care.

Once the danger has been eliminated and the assailant is controlled, you must stop applying force and inflicting injury; otherwise, your actions may no longer qualify as "self-defense" but may appear as delivering punishment to your attacker. Such action is likely to be considered an "unreasonable" application of force.

Legal Status of Self-Defense in a Criminal Context

Self-defense is justified when the degree of violence used to protect yourself is objectively reasonable and proportionate to the threat faced. As an example, the use of deadly force for defensive purposes is permissible in situations of "extreme" danger when you're the victim of a forcible and atrocious crime, or face serious bodily injury or a potentially fatal attack. On the other hand, defense against criminal charges is unjustified, for example, if you claimed the right of self-defense when using deadly force and killed the perpetrator of a minor crime when the criminal did not appear to be a physical threat to anyone. *The right of self-defense is not available to a person who seeks a quarrel with the intent to create a real or apparent necessity of exercising self-defense.*

Self-Defense against Assault   It's lawful for a person who is being assaulted to defend against a physical attack, as long as a reasonable person has grounds for believing, and actually does believe, that bodily injury is about to be inflicted. If that's the case, that person may use all the physical force that she believes to be reasonably necessary and which would appear to a reasonable person, in the same or similar circumstances, to be necessary to prevent the injury that appears to be imminent. You'll be judged by all the information that's known and apparent to you at the time you defend yourself. You won't be judged with 20/20 hindsight. Ultimately, the question will be whether your actions are "objectively reasonable" in light of all of the facts and circumstances confronting you at the time. Justification for self-defense typically cannot be applied to actions committed after a criminal act has taken place. For example, a victim of a sexual assault, after the rape is committed and the rapist leaves the scene of the crime, is not entitled to later seek revenge against the attacker.

The Assailed Person Need Not Retreat   A person who is threatened with a violent attack may exercise the right of self-defense and *need not retreat*. If you exercise your right to self-defense, you may hold your original position and stand your ground and defend yourself by the use of all force and means that would appear to be essential to a reasonable person in a similar situation and with similar knowledge.

Actual Danger Is Not Necessary   "Actual danger" is not necessary as a good reason for acting in self-defense. If you're confronted by the appearance of danger and, as a reasonable person, you possess an actual belief and fear that you're about to suffer bodily injury, and if a reasonable person in a similar situation, seeing and knowing the same facts, would be justified in believing that they were in similar danger, you may use reasonable force to act in self-defense whether the danger itself is authentic or merely apparent.

The Castle Doctrine: Resisting an Intruder upon One's Property

The idea of defending your home, or "castle," is legally known as the Castle Doctrine. You may reasonably defend your home or dwelling against anyone who intends or attempts in a violent manner to enter your home or dwelling and who appears to be a threat to any person in your home or dwelling. In essence, the law presumes that, at the time you used force against an intruder to your residence, you possessed a reasonable fear of imminent peril of death or great bodily injury to you or a member of your family or household. You were thus entitled to use a higher level of force, even deadly force.

Note: States may differ with regard to the specific instances in which the Castle Doctrine is triggered and the degree of retreat or non-deadly force, if any, that is required before deadly force can be used.

The right of self-defense exists only as long as the real or apparent threatened danger continues. So if you're attacked and use force to defend yourself, and you use enough force on the attacker as to leave the attacker seemingly incapable of inflicting further injuries to you, the right to use force in self-defense ends.

Preemptive Self-Defense In some countries as well as a number of U.S. states, the notion of "preemptive" self-defense is limited to only those situations where the threat is imminent. Thus, lawful "preemptive" self-defense is simply the act of landing the first blow in a situation that has reached a point for no de-escalation, resolution, or escape. Many people believe that if the situation is so obvious as to feel assured that violence is inescapable, the defender has a much better probability of surviving by landing the first blow and gaining the immediate upper hand to quickly stop the risk to her person.

Use of Force in Defense of Another It's lawful for you, as a reasonable person, to use force to save another person from harm. If you have grounds for believing, and you actually do believe, that bodily injury is about to be inflicted upon another person, you can use force to protect that individual from attack. In that situation, you may use all force and means that you believe to be reasonably necessary and that would appear to a reasonable person, in the same or similar circumstances, to be necessary to prevent an injury that appears to be imminent. *Old Rule:* The defender stands in the shoes of the person they're defending and if that person doesn't have a right in FACT to use force, then neither does the defender. This is NOT the rule in most states anymore. *New Rule:* If the defender has a reasonable belief that force is necessary to protect a third party, then they're justified in using it, even if the third party is not truly in danger. This is the law in most states now.

Three Golden Rules of Self-Defense

Golden Rule #1: *You may use no greater force than a reasonable person would deem necessary to defend against the threat proffered.*

- What constitutes a threat varies significantly by state, but it always includes physical harm against you.
- If you're a martial arts expert and you KNOW that your assailant is unskilled and unarmed, you can't respond with more force than necessary to eliminate the threat. However, if you don't know the skill level of your assailant, if a reasonable person would THINK that use of your martial arts abilities was necessary

to eliminate the threat (generally the case with most situations involving thugs in dark alleys), it doesn't matter if that is true in FACT. You can and should use your abilities to protect yourself.

- You may not use deadly force unless you reasonably believe that the assailant is using or about to use deadly physical force or is likely to inflict great bodily injury, or is about to commit any other crime (usually burglary, arson, rape, or kidnapping).

Golden Rule #2: *Once the threat is eliminated, you cannot continue to use force.*

- If your assailant retreats, you cannot continue to fight him unless he poses a threat to someone else.
- If you can retreat to avoid confrontation, you may be required to do so, but not necessarily. KNOW THE LAW IN YOUR STATE!
- "True Man" Doctrine: If you didn't initiate the encounter, you're not obligated to retreat, even if you can do so safely, so long as your assailant still poses a threat.
- "Castle Doctrine" (an exception to the retreat rule): If you're in your own home, you're not obligated to retreat, even under a state following the retreat rule.
- The law is unsettled in the area of fighting with someone you share your home with, but many states are considering an exception to the "Castle Doctrine" for cohabitants.

Golden Rule #3: *Don't be the aggressor.*

- "Peterson Doctrine": If you're the initial aggressor, you can't use self-defense as a justification for a use of force, unless you've made a good-faith showing that you wanted to stop fighting.
- If you started a fist fight and the person pulls a knife on you, you probably won't be able to use self-defense as a justification. Most jurisdictions prevent even non-lethal aggressors from using self-defense as a justification if they later use lethal force to defend against lethal force.

Use of Force Reporting Guidelines

Civilians have generally not been trained to write reports that document the general nature of the events that took place during a use of force incident. However, current trends in civil litigation and allegations of excessive force suggest a need to reevaluate that philosophy. Therefore, it may be prudent for those who have been involved in a use of force incident to memorialize it in a truthful, detailed, and comprehensive manner, as described below. You should write the reports in plain English and avoid the use of legalese whenever possible .

Recommended Procedures

- Document the incident in written form as soon as reasonably possible following the incident. The checklist on page 19 may help you to organize your thoughts and to memorialize the use of force incident in a detailed and accurate manner.
- Make sure you give the circumstances resulting in the initial contact; this helps to show reasonable force (i.e., the amount of force, which is objectively reasonable, based on the facts and circumstances confronting you at the time of the event). See "Checklist: Documenting Use of Force" on page 19 for a list of things you should try and detail.
- Describe the assailant, including, but not limited to: sex, race, age, height, weight, build, and clothing worn (any unusual bulges). Also include any factors or observations that indicate the subject was under

Checklist: Documenting Use of Force

Consider all of the factors below:

☐ Describe the nature of the incident concisely and clearly.

☐ Location (remote, obscure, isolated, or high-crime area; lighting, or lack thereof)

☐ Time of incident (late night/early morning)

☐ Document the objective signs that were apparent to you regarding the attacker's emotional, mental, and physical state. Clearly describe why you perceived the subject to be dangerous and how this perception influenced your own mental state (e.g., concerned, fearful, etc.).

☐ Detail any and every aggressive action by the subject directed toward you or third parties. Include verbal threats, gestures, aggressive stance, demeanor, any weapons displayed, and applications of force toward you.

☐ Describe any action by the assailant, such as abrupt movements, attempting to conceal an object, or evasive conduct/responses.

☐ Describe any conversation or orders, if any were made, that you directed to the assailant before the actual physical confrontation. Be sure to describe the assailant's verbal and physical conduct and the reactions (e.g., clenched fists, took a fighting stance, etc.).

☐ Describe the force used to overcome the subject's resistance:

- To the extent possible, identify any techniques and strikes you used and the intended target areas and areas actually struck.

- Describe the force referencing the circumstances that occurred, including any verbalization or directions given to the assailant. Articulate any escalation or de-escalation of force and the attenuating reasons, such as the lack of the combatant's response to the force you used. Describe the combatant's reactions to the force applied in specific detail. This is of critical importance if the force you use is ineffective in stopping the assailant. This will clearly justify why, out of necessity, you had to escalate the level of force used.

- Describe obstacles and difficulties encountered, including fatigue and/or the inability to overcome injuries received from the assailant.

the influence of alcohol or drugs. An evaluation of strength, physical condition, and possible combative skills of the assailant should be articulated. If you've had prior contact with the adversary, this information will be relevant to your state of mind. Also, who else was with the combatant (e.g., friends, relatives) and did their presence pose an additional potential threat to the safety of you or a third party?

- Describe how the conflict ultimately concluded. Indicate the actions that were necessary for you to overcome the attacker's actions, his resistance, how you eliminated the danger posed by the assailant, and what you did to resolve the dangerous circumstances and restore your safety.

Surviving the Encounter

Every two and a half minutes, somewhere in America, someone is sexually assaulted. In fact, both men and women can be victims of sexual assault; however, women are the primary victims of rape, and 9 out of every 10 rape victims were female in 2003. No one should have to suffer the indignity, trauma, and violence of being a victim of sexual assault. You don't have to fight this crime of violence alone. By writing this book, we hope to provide you with important skills in order to fight back; that is, when fighting back is your best option. We also hope to give you tactical options to help you avoid scenarios where you're more vulnerable to being attacked. We'll give you methods so that you become a hardened target. Whatever you do to survive a violent encounter, remember one very important fact: IT'S NOT YOUR FAULT.

Rape, defined for the purpose of this book, is forced sexual intercourse. This definition includes vaginal, anal, or oral penetration. Penetration may be by a perpetrator's body part or an object in his possession. In examining the crime of rape, one out of every six American women has been the victim of an attempted or completed rape in her lifetime (14.8% completed rape; 2.8% attempted rape). It's estimated that 17.7 million American women have been victims of an attempted or completed rape.

It's important to understand that the best self-defense is avoidance—don't be there. While this is ideal, it's certainly not always possible, but any time a confrontation (which may become physical) can be evaded, that is preferred. Physical responses are solutions to problems with no other recourse. In other words, danger is imminent and it cannot be avoided. The "interview process," detailed below, is a vital component in determining whether you should and can avoid a situation.

Our personal demeanor says a lot more about us than we may realize. From the way we walk to the placement of our arms to the position of our shoulders, whether we intend to or not, our body language tells a story. Weak body language relates a weak mentality. With strong posture and a confident walk, you're less likely to be targeted. Assailants will be looking for someone they feel will not fight back. They will study you, and if you look distracted or not confident, these factors can determine whether they decide to attack you or move on. When potential assailants are looking to victimize someone, they go through an "interview process." This is an interview you do not want to pass. The "interview process" consists of four stages.

Stage 1. *Targeting—the observation.* An assailant is looking for someone he feels is weak and will not put up a fight. The last thing he wants is someone who will draw attention to the situation.

Stage 2. *Approach.* Based on what he sees, the assailant has determined that he can get closer. The window is open.

Stage 3. *Conversation.* The assailant will engage in conversation to distract and/or lure you away from where you are. Never go with him!

Stage 4. *The Attack.* The window was never closed and personal boundaries were neither established nor enforced.

Please be aware that these stages can be condensed. There may not be a conversation or the conversation may occur in the approach, assuming the approach is within your vision. This is why awareness is an essential tool in self-defense.

Survival Mindset

Before getting into the details of how to harden yourself as a target, it's important to note that even if you unfortunately pass the four stages of the interview and the physical attack occurs, it doesn't mean that you cannot fight back and survive. This is where your survival mindset kicks in and your Krav Maga skills come into play.

How many times have you heard that it's important to walk with confidence? Do you know what that really means? From a self-defense mindset, it means to convey a consistent image of awareness, inner strength, and knowledge. This image is created through strong and confident body language, eye contact, and voice.

In order to harden yourself as a target, you need to be confident with who you are, know what your boundaries are, and be willing to stand up for yourself by:

- Developing and practicing good AWARENESS skills;
- Developing and practicing good PHYSICAL skills;
- Being cognizant of your BODY LANGUAGE;
- Knowing how to use your VOICE; and with those skills,
- Establishing and enforcing your BOUNDARIES.

Too Close for Comfort

Despite public perception that the victim does not know her rapist, such as in the case of a serial rapist, approximately 73% of rape victims know their assailant, according to the 2005 National Crime Victimization Survey. Although serial rapists receive tremendous coverage in the press, in part because they're relatively less common, be aware that you're more likely to be raped by someone you know.

Studies provide insight as to the relationship between the perpetrator and the rape victim. Approximately 38% of victims are raped by a friend or acquaintance, 28% of victims are raped by someone with whom they share an intimate relationship, and 7% of victims are raped by a relative. In 2% of cases, the relationship is unknown and cannot be determined, and 26% of victims are raped by a stranger.

This combination equals a strong demeanor and presence. To develop and enhance these skills, you must practice them.

The survival mindset (also known as the warrior mindset, or psychological and emotional aspects that allow you to "fight back") is committing your mind to survival. In essence, it's having the willingness to injure or kill another person in order to ensure the preservation of your own life or the life of your loved one(s). With the ability to stay focused and in control, you're more likely to respond immediately with the appropriate level of force to stop the attack and escape. If your first attempt to fight is not effective, NEVER GIVE UP. Until you're safely away, you must keep fighting by whatever means necessary. Let nothing deter you from your survival.

Having the survival mindset is 90% of your self-defense tactics. However, you must put your mindset into practice both visually and physically. Visualize how you would deal with what could happen before it happens. You must also keep practicing your skills in order for them to stay at their best. Developing your mental skills must progress with physical training. If both are not developed together, you may become overly confident and lack the ability to execute a physical response, or you may become extremely skilled physically but mentally unable to exercise your techniques.

Are you an "I can" or an "I can't"? You often hear women say things like, "I can't do that. A man is too strong," or, "I'll never get his hands off of me." If you start out thinking that way, then you're probably right. If you're an "I can't," you must change the way you think. You cannot think of yourself as a victim.

> An officer was shot in a non-fatal area of his body; however, he immediately went to the ground, holding his wound yelling, "I'm going to die, I'm going to die." He didn't listen to anyone who told him that he wasn't going to die and, sadly, he died that evening. It was later determined that his wound was not lethal enough for him to die, but his lack of will to survive, the lack of mental commitment, caused his body to give up.

You must believe you'll survive, no matter what it takes. We must develop our survival mindset and make it our first form of self-defense. It's just like a muscle that needs to be exercised and strengthened. And you must believe you have the right to say "no." You have the right to speak up for yourself and the right to defend yourself, and you need the willingness to do both.

Ladies, you're stronger than you think you are, and oftentimes stronger than men. A woman's greatest strength may not be physical strength, but it's a combination of natural mental strength (survival mindset), physical techniques, and tactics that enables you to get through anything. Why do we drive so hard for everyone else, but when it comes time to fight for ourselves we often don't?

For the right mindset, you must believe you're worth fighting for. You must give yourself permission to fight back.

Now that you believe you have the ability to protect yourself, are you willing to hit back in self-defense? Being willing to stand up for yourself means you may have to get physical. Women have a natural instinct to nurture, not harm others; it's more natural for men to fight. It's important that you realize that defending yourself with a physical action that may harm another human being does not make you wrong, or a bad or evil person. Imagine for a second that the person you love the most is two feet away from you being beaten to death. You wouldn't think twice about doing what needs to be done to save a loved one. So being willing to physically defend yourself means you may need to dig your thumb into a man's eye, slam your fist into his nose, or, in other words: hit, stomp, kick, scratch, spit—whatever it takes to get you free.

Awareness

A vital element of your survival mindset is awareness. Being aware of your environment encompasses more than most realize. It's not just your physical surroundings, but also the people who occupy it. Too often we walk through our day with blinders on. Focusing on our busy schedule, we develop a sort of tunnel vision. Hopefully, the most damage this may cause would be to trip on something or run into someone. However, on that day when we're unknowingly in the path of a potential assailant, the damage could be much worse. With good awareness habits, you can recognize and avoid a dangerous situation before it becomes an altercation.

Your Mental and Physical State   Awareness senses lessen when we're preoccupied by being sick, sleepy, stressed about our schedule, text messaging, etc. This lowered state of readiness is exactly what an assailant is looking for because you appear to be an easy target.

Your Intuition   Listening to your sixth sense, that inner voice, can be one of your most important self-defense skills. If you sense that something is wrong, it is. That gut feeling you get when something is not exactly right is an alert, even if you can't determine exactly what that something is, but you need to learn to listen to that alarm, however vague it may be.

> ### Color Code System of Awareness
>
> Colonel Jeff Cooper developed the Color Code system that's used by most military and police organizations to differentiate different levels of awareness:
>
> **White:** unaware, not paying attention.
>
> **Yellow:** attentive, but relaxed.
>
> **Orange:** focus is directed, there is an immediate potential threat.
>
> **Red:** there is a definite threat.

Your Environment   Know as much as possible ahead of time about the area you'll be visiting. If you're forewarned about dangerous areas, you'll be less likely to traverse them. In areas you frequent (such as where you live and work), think about places where someone could try to hide. Are the areas well lit? When inside a building, know where the exits are located. When outside, know the fastest path toward other people. Recognize changes in your physical environment. Are the lights out? Is there an unusual object in your parking spot that wasn't there when you parked? (It could be a potential ploy used by an attacker to distract your attention.) It's also a good idea to change your routine from time to time. Being a creature of habit can give someone the advantage of predicting where you are at specific times. Have you thought about what things in your everyday environment you might be able to use as a weapon or shield? A pen? A chair? Be aware that common objects can be used to strike or protect you from being struck.

Peripheral vision is a great tool. It encompasses all that's visible to the eye outside the central area of focus (i.e., your side vision). With mindful practice of this vision, it can become a natural resource of observation. Here's an exercise to help develop your awareness skills:

> *Start by sitting in your living room. Look forward and, without turning your head, start naming off what you see to the side of you. This will be relatively simple due to the fact that you're already familiar with the items in your home. The next time you're in a restaurant or another less-familiar place, do the same exercise. Look forward and name what the people around you are doing or*

wearing by using your peripheral vision. Before you know it, you'll pick up on things you never previously noticed and, more importantly, the more you practice using your peripheral vision, the more automatic it will become.

Become more in touch with what you see. We often look to see where we are, but don't actually see much of what we look at. Let's go back to the restaurant exercise. Once you sit down, try to recall what you saw from the time you entered until the time you sat down. How many people were wearing baseball caps? How many children did you pass by? Pick any detail you can and name it.

Current Crime in Your Area   Know the statistics for crime as well as the types of crime that occur in your area.

Body Language

Body language communicates how comfortable you feel about yourself. In self-defense, confident body language conveys a clear signal that you're aware and not an easy target.

The first phase of an attack (in the interview) is often called the "targeting" stage; the attacker is searching for a victim. During this phase, portraying (or having) confident and relaxed body language is critical. Just walking with a purpose could discourage an attack: Keep your head up, look forward, and drop your shoulders (don't hunch them). Walk with a relaxed step (not too long or short), and keep your hands out of your pockets.

Compare these two images in your mind: a woman looking down at the ground as she walks down the street or across a parking lot, and the one just described. Who's an easier target? Who appears vulnerable? These changes are small, but they make an enormous difference, especially to a potential attacker.

Very often we wear our moods on our sleeves. If you're out and about and have had a bad day, or are feeling sick or tired, don't let this change your body language or your awareness level. Stay in Yellow (see "Color Code System of Awareness" on page 23). Knowing that emotions can affect our physical appearance, if you're in a threatening situation with a potential assailant, you don't want to show that you may be nervous or scared. Someone looking for a victim to attack will be watching for any sign that you're nervous or scared, and see that as a sign to proceed. The chances are high that you'll be adrenalized and scared, but you must not let them see it. Hide it by staying calm, looking them in the eyes, and saying what you want them to do.

Boundaries

We have both emotional and physical boundaries, and we need to be willing to enforce them no matter what type of situation we're faced with. Too often women allow boundaries to be crossed in order to avoid being rude or hurting someone's feelings. However, you need to realize that it's much better to go home safe and have someone think of you as a "crazy person" or a "bitch" than to take the chance of not going home at all.

Emotional Boundaries

Recognizing what affects us emotionally is fundamental to creating the right mindset for defending ourselves. Knowing what bothers you (i.e., what behaviors from other people you'll accept and what behaviors you'll not accept on an emotional level) is one of the key aspects of setting emotional boundaries. Recognizing your emotional boundaries is quite simple: If it doesn't feel right, then it's not right. If you're uncomfortable with a situa-

Krav Maga Training Saved My Life

On a summer afternoon in the Koreatown section of Los Angeles, my life was changed forever. As I was walking to my car in a subterranean garage, I looked up after hearing a strange sound. A beat-up van with two men was slowly backing out of a space. I noticed these men were staring at me. As the van drove past me, I heard the van door open and close and that was when I was grabbed from behind.

I immediately turned into him and reacted explosively. My Krav Maga training kicked in. I grabbed a hold of him and proceeded to scream as I delivered powerful knees to his torso. I heard tires screech. The driver left his crime partner behind. My vision narrowed, but my punches and knees didn't stop striking my attacker.

I awoke in a police car, face down and handcuffed in the backseat. My attacker was also in custody. I yelled for someone to listen to me and told a patrol officer that I was defending myself by using Krav Maga.

Luckily, the entire incident had been captured on security cameras and my attacker was charged with several serious felony crimes. I was thankful that before the attack, I went to Krav Maga to work out and had been training on "ground and pound" drills with a kick shield. The police officers were extremely happy that I knew Krav Maga and had been able to defend myself. The fact that Krav Maga helped save my life inspired me to teach other women how to defend themselves. I'm now teaching women to use Krav Maga in order to survive violent, stressful confrontations.

tion, then it's likely that your emotional boundary is being crossed. This is a physical feeling that manifests in a number of different ways or places in the body. It's different for everyone. Try this exercise:

> Find a coworker or an acquaintance (try not to use a family member or friend; your physical boundaries will be different with someone you're close with, and the exercise may not work). First, get their permission to do this exercise. There's no physical contact, just some boundary crossing. While doing the exercise, do your best to refrain from talking or giggling. Stay focused and in touch with your body and what you may feel. Stand facing one another. Take a step forward so you're standing toe to toe. REALLY stand TOE to TOE. Hold that position for 20 seconds. Stay silent, and focus on what you feel. Now go do it, and come back when you're done.

So what did you feel? Did you feel tightness in your shoulders, tension in your neck, or maybe your chest felt heavy? Perhaps a little nauseated, or a tightness in your stomach? Weak in the knees? You need to know what alerts you. You may not be able to describe it, but you may feel it and need to know the feeling.

These feelings are a chemical reaction in your body telling you that something isn't right. These feelings are your survival instincts. Know them. Utilize them. If something is making you uncomfortable, trust your instincts. Acknowledge what your emotional boundaries are, speak up for yourself, or take action to establish and enforce them.

Physical Boundaries

It's normal to have different physical boundaries in different settings. When you're at home with your family, it's not uncommon to sit side by side on the couch, with your body close enough to be touching the person next to you. However, if you're sitting in an office waiting room on a couch next to a stranger, it's likely you'll keep a reasonable distance between the two of you. In our day-to-day life, we generally allow people we know to be fairly close to us. But even when it comes to strangers in a crowded public place that seems safe simply because there are others around (such as a mall, bar, or lobby of a restaurant), it's still a good idea to be aware of your distance and others' mannerisms.

You should keep a safe distance between you and a stranger. A good guideline for a safe distance (wherever possible) is two-arm's length reach from a stranger. That distance allows you to hear what a person is saying, as well as provides you a reactionary gap should you need to effectively respond. Distance equals time and time equals safety, and that could be the difference between being safe or being the target of an attack.

Verbal Boundaries

Say what you mean in order to enforce your boundaries, such as "Leave now!" not "Can you please just go away?" or "Just leave me alone." Make your point clearly and concisely. The more words you use, the more likely that your message will get lost. Avoid "please" and "thank you" in situations where you're establishing and enforcing your boundaries. It's okay to be polite as a tactical choice of words, but don't qualify or give reason for your statement. Remember, it's not what you say but how you say it, and being rude or angry when you're dealing with a threatening situation can quickly make it worse. Know what you want, state it clearly and directly, and stick to it.

Know Your Triggers

Triggers are products of some past event. A trigger could be a smell, a sound, or a physical object. Triggers can affect you physically and mentally. The key is to remember that the situation that contains the trigger is not happening now; it already occurred in the past, and you need to remain focused on the present. Your safety depends on it. You don't want a trigger to overtake your ability to stay focused in a potentially dangerous encounter with a stranger. Take three deep breaths. Breathing deeply and fully signals your parasympathetic system to respond by generating a sense of relaxation.

If you have to say something more than twice, they're not listening. Repeat yourself and stand your ground, but understand you may need to change the way you're saying it. Be firmer and/or louder. Always remember that if you can leave a situation safely, leave. Don't defer the "no"! By putting off something to another time, instead of definitively saying "no," you'll just have to deal with it another day.

You need to be okay with saying "no" today. Repeat if necessary. Don't apologize too much. (Women are especially bad about this.) Interrupt the person. You don't need to be polite if they aren't listening to you. Plus, interrupting them will serve to distract and redirect their energy.

Imagine that you're leaving the store late at night with an armful of groceries. A man approaches you and asks to assist you with putting your groceries in the vehicle. The way you use your voice can determine whether or not he accepts your reply. For example: "No, thank you, I can handle it?" (with uncertainty or simply not enough strength in your voice) versus "No, thank you! I can handle it." As a general note, when speaking with a stranger you want to put yourself in a higher state of awareness. Now, this isn't to say go immediately "red" and walk around in a fighting stance, but instead just move your state of awareness from yellow to orange. This state is where we should be when we're out in public.

Verbalization

Our voice is a powerful instrument and the gateway to communication. Babies don't understand how to formulate words, but instinctively cry to communicate that they need something. They may not know why they're crying, but they know that they're uncomfortable in some manner. With growth comes the use of words and specific communication. A person's needs, likes, and dislikes can now be communicated: I am hungry. I need to use the bathroom. I don't want to go!

Knowing what is liked or disliked starts with emotions. Emotions exist naturally and, with the development of speech, we start to combine them to convey what we feel. This is conveyed in the tone, inflection, and volume (TIV) of our voice. *Tone* essentially establishes the context of the conversation. Tone can be described as the quality of a person's voice—angry, nervous, scared, confident, commanding. *Inflection* is the rise and fall of voice pitch used for expression. The way you change your voice affects the message that you convey in a situation. Does what you say sound like a question or a statement? *Volume* is the level and quality of sound in your voice that is the primary psychological correlate of physical strength or lack thereof. How loudly you speak in a situation can positively or negatively affect the outcome.

The way we speak our words can change the meaning. Example:

> Can you close the door?
> Can YOU close the door!

Most often the ability to combine the correct tone, inflection, and volume (TIV) with your words is natural and easy in everyday life. But when we're in an uncomfortable situation, our emotions can get the best of us and cause the combination to be off-balance. Although the words we choose are important, the way we say them can be more important. Our body language also plays a big part in the message we convey. A great example of how all of these pieces (voice [TIV], words, body language) play a role in our demeanor is to observe how a child responds to a situation. It's so easy to tell when children are mad, sad, or happy. They absolutely wear their emotions on their sleeves.

Your collective demeanor (body language, eye contact, facial expression, voice [TIV]) should match the message you want to convey in all situations.

1. Body Language: Posture should be relaxed, but alert and confident. Stand with your feet slightly staggered (one foot slightly ahead of the other) about shoulder-width apart, with your weight evenly distributed over both feet. Keep your back straight, your head up, and your hands up in front of you in some fashion. Avoid folding your arms or having your hands in your pockets. Also avoid shifting your weight from side to side or pacing because this conveys you're nervous.

2. Eye Contact: Maintain eye contact—not a hard gaze, which can be threatening, but look people in the eye. Avoid averting your gaze, which can be interpreted as an expression of fear, lack of interest, disregard, or rejection.

3. Facial Expression: Keep a relaxed face and a composed expression. A calm, attentive expression reduces hostility. Conversely, looking bored or disapproving could increase hostility.

4. Voice: Correct use of tone, inflection, and volume is essential to convey the right message of confidence or assertiveness as needed.

Verbal Tactics

When we interact with a friend or family member, we usually know their background and personal mannerisms and, therefore, we're generally familiar with how they'll respond in a given situation. When dealing with strangers, however, we don't have this knowledge, so we never know when or why someone may turn on us. This is where the tactical use of our voice is necessary.

By recognizing your situation and implementing the correct combination of your voice (TIV), words, and body language, the appropriate response can be communicated. It's important to be able to set verbal boundaries to protect yourself. Be sure you're sending the same message with all of your tools.

For example, you're approached by a coworker who asks you out to dinner. You respond by selecting all of the correct words, telling him that you're very flattered but do not date people within your work environment. You may have a confident body position but the inflection in your voice and the lack of eye contact are telling him "maybe" versus a definitive "no."It's common to not want to offend or hurt someone's feelings so we're polite even when it may offend us or cause undue stress. You can be polite and still say "no." If that person truly wants to be your friend, he'll respect your wishes.

De-escalation

De-escalation tactics are an important self-defense strategy used to defuse a potentially dangerous situation. The first and only objective in de-escalation is to reduce the level of anger/agitation so that a calmer discussion becomes possible. Reasoning with an enraged person is not possible. De-escalation skills are an important tool when dealing with people who are highly agitated, frustrated, angry, fearful, or intoxicated. These may ordinarily be peaceful individuals who are responding to an unusual or extreme circumstance; or, they may in fact be individuals with disruptive or potentially violent personalities. By controlling yourself and using tactical communication, you can reduce the increasing threat in a situation.

The goal of de-escalation is to reduce the likelihood of the situation transitioning from a verbal altercation to physical violence. De-escalation can be achieved by developing a rapid rapport and a sense of connection with an agitated person. De-escalation, although a verbal tactic, consists not only of verbal techniques, but also psychological (emotions) and nonverbal (body language) techniques. De-escalation is a tactic of altering your demeanor to fit the circumstances. To use de-escalation as a self-defense tactic, you need to adapt your demeanor to the situation at hand and overcome or control your personal emotions. Here are some additional tactics to put into your toolbox:

1. Body Language: Have a confident body posture, but don't look too aggressive. Pay close attention to your emotions, and be cautious to avoid tensing up your shoulders, neck, hands, or face. If you're unable to compose your emotions, they can (and likely will) be felt by the aggravated person and may cause your de-escalation efforts to fail, despite using an appropriate tone and words. Stand relatively still, avoiding sudden jerky or excessive movements. Make sure to keep your hand gestures to a minimum. Basically, think similarly to how you would deal with an angry dog.

2. Voice: You generally want to keep your voice calm, firm, and low while speaking slowly and evenly. The tone, inflection, and volume of your voice can increase or decrease the other person's anxiety and agitation. However, if the person is yelling, you may need to initially speak in a louder tone in order to be heard, and then guide them to a softer and slower pace.

- *Listen actively.* Gather information by asking questions to develop a rapport, if possible under the circumstances, and gather information in order to begin to guide the communication in a less volatile direction.
- *Acknowledge their feelings.* Some agitated people are unable to problem solve until their feelings are dealt with. By acknowledging their feelings, it often lets them know that they're being heard.
- *Communicate clearly by explaining your intentions and conveying your expectations.* Repeat yourself as much as necessary until you're heard.

Certain behaviors have been found to escalate agitated people:

- Ignoring the person
- Making threats
- Hurtful remarks and/or name calling
- Arguing
- Commanding or shouting
- Invading personal space
- Threatening gestures with your arms or hands, such as finger wagging or pointing

Keep in mind that our natural instincts when in an aggressive or potentially violent encounter are to fight, flight, or freeze. However, in using de-escalation, we can't do any of these. We must appear centered and calm even when we're terrified. Therefore, these techniques must be practiced before they're needed, so that they can become second nature.

But keep in mind: It's always important that you trust your instincts. If you feel that de-escalation is not working, STOP! You'll know within as little as a few minutes to sometimes only a few seconds if it's beginning to work. If not, tell the person to leave, escort him/her to the door, call for help, walk away, and/or call the police.

Tactical Tips for Women

This section provides a plethora of information that may seem intuitive but can be easy to neglect when you're busy or life simply "takes over." In the most general terms, these tips can be boiled down to "be aware," "be vigilant," and "if something feels wrong, it likely is." However, there are many specifics here worth committing to memory and sharing with friends and family. Hopefully by following these tips, your need for the techniques shown throughout this book will be greatly minimized.

When you're out and about:

- Be aware of your surroundings. Knowing where you are and who's around you may help you to find a way to get out of a bad situation.
- Always be vigilant and remain mentally alert and aware of your surroundings. Plan your route and know what "safe" places are along it, such as police stations, fire stations, hospitals, etc.

- Try to avoid isolated areas. It's more difficult to get help if no one's around.
- Walk with confidence, purpose, and evoke a strong presence. Even if you don't know where you're going, act like you do.
- Trust your instincts. If a situation or location feels unsafe or uncomfortable, it probably isn't the best place to be. If you feel uncomfortable or threatened, leave the situation and go to a safe place.
- Try not to overload yourself with packages, books, or bags, as this can make you appear more vulnerable.
- Make sure your cell phone is with you, charged, and that it's easily accessible. Be certain to have important numbers programmed into your cell phone. However, if you lose your cell phone, or if it's taken from you or destroyed, it's advisable to commit all of the important phone numbers to memory beforehand.
- Establish a code word so that family, friends, etc., know when to call for help.
- Don't allow yourself to be isolated with someone you don't trust or someone you don't know. Avoid walking alone whenever possible.

- When walking (or driving), take major public streets and paths rather than less-populated shortcuts, and avoid dimly lit places. Make sure to talk to authorities if lights need to be installed in an area.
- Carry a small noisemaker (like a whistle) and/or flashlight on your keychain.
- Avoid putting music headphones in both ears so that you can be more aware of your surroundings, especially if you're walking alone.
- Be conscious of exits or other escape routes.
- Keep cash and some change with you at all times just in case you need to use a pay phone.
- Have a backup plan in case the first fails.
- Be aware of your routine and, if possible, try to alter it sometimes.
- While driving, keep all of the car doors locked.
- Try not to wait until the last minute to fill your gas tank; always keep it at least half full if you can.
- Have extra car necessities (oil, jumper cables, etc.).
- Have your keys out and in a ready position when you approach your car to unlock it.
- Should you use public transportation, be alert at bus or subway stops when waiting for it to arrive and make it your practice to know the bus or subway schedule to avoid waiting for a long time at a stop. Plan to use the busiest, best-lighted stops/stations possible.
- If someone is bothering you on the bus or subway, tell the driver or use the emergency signal.

- If you feel you're being followed and you're uneasy about getting off at your usual stop, stay on until the next stop or wait until the next safest stop.

At social events:

- When attending social events, go to the party with a group of trusted friends. Make an effort to arrive together. Keep an eye on one another and be sure to check in with each other throughout the event, and leave together.
- Always know where you are. For example, know the address and phone number of the location, and be sure to let someone else, preferably someone not attending the party with you, know about your where-abouts. Knowing your location and where you are within that location may help you to summon help and find a way out of a dangerous situation.
- Be sure to trust your intuition. If you feel uneasy or that your security is compromised in any way, it may be your instincts trying to warn you. Trust your instincts and be cautious—take appropriate steps to restore your feeling of security.
- NEVER leave your drink unattended while at a party. If you've been distracted in any way by socializing, talking, dancing, using the restroom, or making a phone call, and during that time, you left your drink unat-tended, make it a rule to ALWAYS get a new one.
- Don't accept drinks from people you don't know well or trust. At parties, don't drink from open punch bowls or other large, common containers being shared. Remember, drugs used to facilitate rape cannot be tasted or smelled.
- If you suspect you (or a friend) have been drugged, contact law enforcement immediately by calling 911 (in most areas of the U.S.).
- Keep your drink secured at all times. Cover it. It's easy to inconspicuously place a small pill or a vial of liquid while you're in possession of your drink.
- If you feel extremely tired or unjustifiably drunk, you may have been drugged. Leave the area with your trusted friends immediately.

At home:

- While at home, keep all the doors to your home locked at all times and don't prop open your doors or win-dows, even during hot summer evenings. Periodically change the locks on the doors and the windows to your home, especially if you've had construction and repair workers in your home or if you've shared your keys with a friend or significant other with whom you're no longer close.
- Be sure to install and use a quality security system that is connected to doors leading to your home, as well as to the door and windows of your bedroom. Also, be sure to have panic buttons throughout your residence and, most notably, in your bedroom, so that you have the ability to activate the alarm system, whether it's a loud or silent alarm. Be sure your alarm system is properly permitted and is directly linked to a professional security service, as well as with your local law-enforcement agency.
- Install an outside lighting system around the perimeter of your property. It's essential that this system be equipped with motion detectors. This may help you to surmise where an intruder is located on your property.
- Always keep your window, blinds, and curtains closed at night.
- Keep car doors locked, even in your own driveway or garage.

What to Do If You're Raped or
Assaulted

Most rapes do not result in physical injuries. A lack of such injuries should not deter you from reporting. We hope you'll decide to report your attack to the police. While there's no way to change what happened to you, you can seek justice and help prevent it from happening to someone else. Reporting your rape or attack to the police is essential in stopping future sexual assaults: Every time a rapist is put in jail, it prevents him from committing another attack. This is the most effective tool to prevent future rapes. However, in the end, the decision of whether or not to report is up to you.

Many victims say that reporting is the last thing they want to do right after being attacked. This is perfectly understandable—reporting can seem invasive, time consuming, and difficult. However, there are many good reasons to report, and some victims say that reporting has aided their recovery and helped them regain a feeling of control.

If you choose to report your rape, call 911, or ask a friend or family member to make the call for you. Or, if you wish, you can visit a hospital emergency room or your own doctor and ask them to call the police for you. If you visit the emergency room and tell the nurse that you've been raped, the hospital will usually perform a sexual assault forensic examination. In most areas, if you wish for someone to accompany you, the local rape crisis center can help. Call 800-656-HOPE to contact the center in your area.

Why It's Important to Report the Crime

Slightly more than one half of rape victims don't report the crime. The good news, however, is that reporting is up substantially in the last decade. The most common reason that victims give for not reporting the rape (23%) is that the rape is a "personal matter." Another 16% of victims say that they fear reprisal, while about 6% don't report because they believe that the police are biased.

The FBI ranks rape as the second-most violent crime, second only to murder. Every rape is a very serious crime that should be prosecuted, even if no physical injuries occur during the assault. Sixty percent of rapes/sexual assaults are not reported to the police, which means those rapists never spend a day in prison for the crimes that they've committed. Factoring in unreported rapes, only about 6% of rapists ever serve a day in jail.

The Legal System—No One Can Make You Testify If You Change Your Mind

While there is generally no time limit on reporting your rape to the police, to maximize the chances of an arrest and successful prosecution, it's important that you report the incident to the police as soon as possible after the rape. If you aren't sure what to do, it's better to report now and decide what to do later. That way, the evidence is preserved in case you decide that you wish to pursue prosecution. Some states have statutes of limitations that bar prosecutions after a certain number of years.

Understandably, many people aren't ready to make the decision about prosecution immediately after an attack. It's normal to want time to think about the decision and talk it over with friends and family. If you think you might want to pursue prosecution, but haven't decided for sure, you should still report your rape to the police, while the evidence is still present and your memory is still detailed. The district attorney will decide whether or not to pursue prosecution; however, it's unusual for cases to proceed without the cooperation of the victim. If the district attorney does decide to pursue prosecution, the chance of success will be much higher if you followed the procedures outlined in this chapter.

One more thing to consider is that if you're planning to apply for compensation through your state's Victim Compensation Fund, you'll likely first have to report your attack to the police to be eligible. Contact your local rape crisis center at 800-656-HOPE to learn about the rules in your state.

Things to Do to Preserve Evidence

In the immediate aftermath of a sexual assault, the most important thing you can do is to make sure that you get to a safe place. This can be your house, a friend's home, or somewhere safe with a family member. When safety has been achieved, it's imperative for you to seek medical attention, and it's highly recommended that you undergo a forensic examination to collect evidence.

The preservation of DNA evidence is extremely important in the process of identifying an attacker or rapist. This is particularly true in cases where the attacker is a stranger to the victim. DNA evidence is an integral part of a law-enforcement investigation and is often used to strengthen the case and to show that the defendant was the cause of the sexual assault.

You should make every effort to save anything that might contain the perpetrator's DNA, therefore you shouldn't:

- Bathe or shower
- Use the restroom
- Change clothes
- Comb hair
- Clean up the crime scene
- Move anything the offender may have touched

Even if you haven't yet decided to report the crime, receiving a medical exam and keeping the evidence safe from damage will increase the chances that the police can access and test the evidence in the future. After the

Guidelines for Victims of Sexual Assault

To reiterate the material covered in this chapter, here are some guidelines of what you should do if you ever find yourself the victim of a sexual assault:

- *Find a safe environment*—anywhere away from the attacker. Ask a trusted friend to stay with you for moral support.
- *Know that what happened was not your fault* and that now you should do what is best for you.
- *Report the attack to the police by calling 911.* You can also call the National Sexual Assault Hotline at 800-656-HOPE to speak to a counselor who can help you understand the process.
- *Preserve evidence of the attack.* Do NOT bathe or brush your teeth.
- *Write down all of the details that you can recall* about the attack and the attacker.
- *Ask the hospital to conduct a rape kit exam* to preserve forensic evidence.
- *If you suspect you were drugged, ask that a urine sample be collected.* The sample will need to be analyzed later on by a forensic lab.

If you know that you'll never report, still consider these steps:

- *Get medical attention.* Even with no physical injuries, it's important to determine the risks of STDs and pregnancy.
- *Call the National Sexual Assault Hotline for free confidential counseling: 800-656-HOPE.*
- *Recognize that healing from rape takes time.* Give yourself the time you need.

medical examination is performed and all of the evidence is collected and stored in the rape kit, you'll be able to take a shower, brush your teeth, etc.

Get Psychological Help Whether You Report or Not

Regardless of whether or not you report your rape, it's imperative that you seek psychological help to get you through this difficult time. Whether you call a sexual assault hotline, seek counseling, or simply talk to a friend or loved one about what you've been through, psychological help is an essential part of the recovery process. Remember, you're not alone in this and you'll always have someone available to talk to and to help you.

If you're in need of psychological help, please refer to RAINN (Rape, Abuse & Incest National Network) at www.rainn.org for services that are available to you.

Know that it's never too late to call. Even if the attack happened years ago, the National Sexual Assault Hotline (800-656-HOPE) or the National Sexual Assault Online Hotline can still help.

TECHNIQUES

Getting Started

Once you've made the decision to begin your Krav Maga training, there are several things to keep in mind to ensure the best training experience. Hopefully, you'll be able to find a certified Krav Maga Worldwide instructor in your area (see page 9 for more information). Your instructor will be sure to address the following issues.

Preparing for a Training Session

In order to get the most out of your sessions, you should be prepared, physically and mentally, for the training. You should consult your physician to ensure that this type of training is suitable for you.

As part of your physical preparations, you should consider a diet that will optimize your session. Eating a carbo-hydrate-rich meal three to four hours before training will serve to fuel your body. Eating an easily digestible snack an hour or so beforehand should give you the added boost to get you started. Since most Krav Maga sessions last an hour, water is ideal for your hydration. It's important to drink water, not only during your training, but throughout the day.

A typical Krav Maga Worldwide class consists of a warm-up, combatives training, self-defense training, and drills. Warm-ups are designed to prepare the body both physically and mentally for the hard training ahead, but you know your body better than anyone. If you have problem areas that need extra attention (such as stretching), you should take the initiative to address this before your session begins. It's also imperative that you notify your instructor of any injuries that you may have.

You should also spend some preparation time on getting ready mentally. As is done on the physical side, your certified instructor will employ techniques to do just this, but you should spend some time thinking about the training and your training goals before you begin the class. Simply showing up to train is a big step, but coming in with specific goals in mind, and the understanding that maximum effort will produce maximum results, will provide you with the best training experience.

Safety in Training

While your certified instructor and licensed training facility will go to great lengths to produce a safe training experience, the onus is often on the student to ensure personal safety and the safety of training partners. Krav Maga Worldwide classes are designed to prepare students for self-defense in the real world, against real-life attacks. The recommended training attire reflects this goal, while also making considerations for optimal training. Lightweight nylon pants or knee-length shorts are preferred, along with a T-shirt and cross-training-type shoes that provide support for moving in all directions.

Krav Maga Worldwide training centers attract people from all walks of life, with varying experiences, backgrounds, and training goals. It's important to understand and respect these factors when training. During the initial stages of your training, when partnering, you should try to partner with someone of similar size. This may not always be possible, so considering potential size and strength differences to ensure the safety of everyone is vital to a productive training atmosphere. While students are there to better themselves, peripheral goals should include bettering the others in the class. Also, while we want to engender a realistic training experience, this should not be done at the unnecessary risk of injury. If you feel a student does not wholly understand how to train safely, speak with your instructor. Once you've gained experience in the system, you'll be encouraged to train with partners who are larger than you.

Your training environment should be controlled as much as possible. If training at a licensed facility, this should be a normal part of business, but you should do your part to be diligent in understanding inherent or potential dangers. You should remove obstacles (such as chairs, tables, objects with sharp edges) that are not needed for the training at hand. You should also remove jewelry (earrings, necklaces, rings) and watches that may cause injury to yourself or others. You should check equipment to verify its integrity. If training outdoors, be sure to scan the area and remove items that may be hazardous. If you're not training at a licensed facility, you should be sure to have a first-aid kit on hand during your sessions.

Recommended Training Equipment

Certain items are essential for the ideal training experience. For combative training, there are several types of training pads that will serve to enhance your training. These pads have one important thing in common: They allow you to strike a solid object in order to condition yourself to replicate striking an adversary in a fight. Delivering strikes to the air may be of some benefit, but striking and meeting the resistance of a pad reflects the contact you'll experience in a fight for your life.

Kickshield

The *punch or "tombstone" pad* is very versatile. Most upper body combatives, as well as some kicks, can be performed on this pad.

The *kickshield pad* is ideal for practicing many of the stronger kicks used in Krav Maga. It's also used for practicing knees and is prevalent in many training drills.

Focus mitts are used for intermediate and advanced combative training, particularly punches.

Focus mitts

In order to train hard and minimize injuries, there are several essential pieces of gear. Handwraps, gloves, and mouthpieces are at the top of the list. However, it's also important to train, at times, without this gear. This should be done only in a controlled and supervised training environment.

There are many styles and sizes of gloves, which vary according to training goals. For basic Krav Maga training, 12- to 16-ounce boxing gloves are ideal for heavy punching and controlled sparring. These gloves may be worn with or without handwraps. While there are inexpensive options out there, higher-quality gloves are recommended because they last longer and generally provide a greater degree of safety for your hands and wrists. Krav Maga gloves, as well as other equipment, can be found at www.kravmaga.com.

If you plan to engage in heavy punching or sparring, you may want to consider wrapping your hands. Handwraps are designed to provide wrist and knuckle protection during hard punching. For a detailed account of how you should wrap your hands, please visit www.glovesandhandwraps.com, a site run by Revgear Sports.

Striking Basics

It's imperative that you learn to use the different tools of your body to inflict damage on someone who seeks to harm you. The approach to surviving a violent encounter is simple: Eliminate a threat posed by an attacker and then neutralize the attacker. Various parts of your body are ideal for inflicting damage on another person. This section will show you how to do so.

Training Positions

In an ideal world, it's generally preferred to strike with the "strong side" back (i.e., a right-handed defender has right hand/leg back and left hand/leg forward), but the truth is, this is a luxury. So, for this book, we'll designate which hand/leg is forward or back, but only for illustrative purposes. A prepared "stance" is not assumed, since it's probable that you'll be caught unaware; therefore, it's important to train from various positions. Defenders should be less concerned with any specific "posture" and more concerned with striking aggressively.

Neutral position is for training purposes. This position isn't a stance in the traditional sense, but rather the absence of a dedicated stance, used to put the trainee in a position of disadvantage. While this position can, and at higher levels should, vary, for beginners, it generally looks something like this:

- Your feet should be approximately shoulder-width apart (or less); they should not be wider than the shoulders when standing neutral.
- Arms should hang along the sides or be up in a ready position.

Fighting stance is the position you should adopt when preparing for a confrontation or once a confrontation has begun.

Foot position:
- Assuming you're right-handed, your left leg is forward, with a slight bend in your knees and your weight centered and in the balls of your feet (not heels).
- Your right (rear) heel is slightly elevated and not on the ground.

Neutral position

- Your feet should be slightly wider than shoulder width apart and about one step deep (from front to back). The depth and width will vary from individual to individual. If your feet are too narrow, you won't be stable. If your feet are too wide, they can inhibit movement. Your goal is to feel balanced for easy mobility forward, backward, and side to side.
- The toes of both feet should generally point forward.

Hand position:
- Your hands should be up with fingertips at eyebrow level.
- Your elbows should be held in fairly close to your body.
- Your hands should be relaxed (not in fists), and approximately 6 to 10 inches from your face. This will vary depending on the distance of your opponent. If your opponent is closer, your hands should be closer; if farther away, your hands can be farther away from your face.
- Your shoulders should be relatively square to the opponent (i.e., don't turn sideways).
- Your chin should be tucked and your eyes forward.

If you're left-handed, perform a mirror image of the stance (i.e., with your right foot forward, etc.).

Fighting stance

A less-aggressive stance can be taken when you're unsure of a threat level and want to be prepared without escalating a situation.

- Your feet are the same as fighting stance, with perhaps a little less bend in your knees.
- Your hands are in a position of readiness similar to a fighting stance but less obvious to the opponent. *Example:* You may have your hands up but lower than your face, clasped together or open.

Less-aggressive stance

Preferred Target Areas

When defending, attacking vulnerable areas of the attacker's body is key. The majority of the areas are highlighted in the image below.

While these are certainly not the only targets available, these areas are generally preferred because they're typically soft tissue, have many nerve endings, and/or are joints, which are weaker than parts that are "joined." Such areas, as you can see, are found all over the body, making one or more accessible in virtually any self-defense situation. All of these areas may be used for inflicting damage.

Note: It's usually preferred to use "softer" striking surfaces against "harder" targets (e.g., heel of palm to back of head) and "harder" striking surfaces against "softer" targets (e.g., elbow to throat). However, think of this more as a guideline than a rule. If in doubt, hit what you can with what you have.

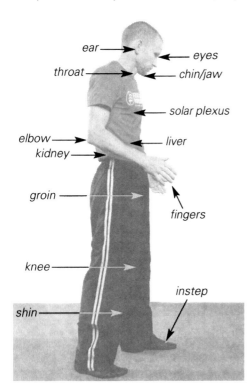

Preferred target areas

crown of head

mouth of hand

fingertips

heel of palm

knuckles

bottom of fist

elbow

forearm

knee

shin

bottom of heel

ball of foot

instep

Ideal striking surfaces

Striking Surfaces

For the purposes of this book, you should consider virtually the entire body, and all of its "parts," as weapons. That said, there are surfaces on the body that tend to be more effective for striking. The most ideal striking surfaces are illustrated above.

Personal Weapons

The term "personal weapon" refers to one's natural weapons. In other words, this involves using different parts of the body, such as the striking surfaces noted above, to cause damage to an attacker. This section will cover the most efficient methods for using these body parts, as well as the most effective and available targets.

Although the personal weapons we detail are some of the most preferred and effective methods of causing damage to an attacker, there are others that are certainly worth mentioning:

- **Gouging:** This literally refers to digging at the eyes with the thumbs. It's extremely effective from very close range.
- **Biting:** While this may seem pretty cut and dry, it's important to note that the goal of biting is to create an opportunity for a more devastating attack. Biting is very effective in creating a "flinch" response, causing the attacker to make an adjustment and therefore creating an opening for the defender.
- **Grabbing and tearing:** Using the fingers and hands to grasp and rip at the attacker's body (groin, face, hair, skin, etc.) can create space and opportunity as well as inflict pain.
- **Leverage on joints and breaking:** Here we're primarily talking about attacking small, vulnerable joints, like the fingers. Holding the fingers at the base and explosively taking them in unnatural directions is very painful and can be debilitating.

Straight Punches

A straight punch extends forward in a straight line from your shoulder to the target. It can be delivered at any angle on a horizontal or vertical plane, and be made with either hand. Since the shortest distance between two points is a straight line, a straight punch is the fastest, most direct, and least detectable way to send a punch to the targeted area. In most cases, for a right-handed person, the rear or right punch will have more power than the front hand (left, in this case) because the rear hip can pivot forward to create more power.

The straight punch can be used to distract, stun, injure, or knock out your attacker, giving you the ability to eliminate the threat and the time to escape from the danger zone. Strike to whatever vulnerable target is open. If the attacker's arms are up high, you should strike low; if his hands are down low, you should strike high. A sound strategy is to create openings. For instance, if the attacker's hands are up and covering his face, strike to vulnerable areas that are low. This will generally cause the attacker to drop his hands, opening targets to the face, throat, and chin.

Making a Fist

1–4 Roll your fingers tightly so that there's no space. Seal your thumb tightly over your fingers near the first knuckle. Do NOT put your thumb inside your fingers!

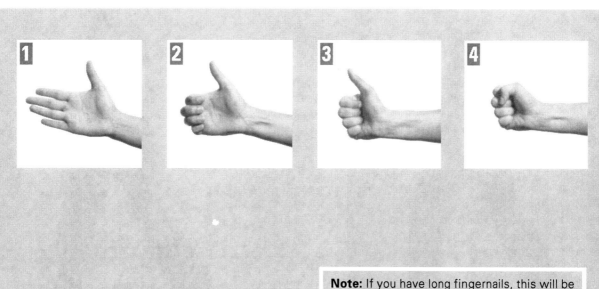

Note: If you have long fingernails, this will be difficult and likely uncomfortable. In such a case, open-hand strikes (such as page 48) may be preferred. Or cut your nails.

STRIKING BASICS **45**

Starting Position

Preferred Target Areas: chin, jaw, throat, nose

Striking Surface: first two knuckles (index and middle finger) of the fist

Starting Position: fighting stance

1 Primarily driving with your legs, with the support of your core, send your fist forward. Drive the punch forward by pushing the ball of your back foot against the floor. Push off the floor to place more power in the punch. As your hips and shoulders rotate, extend your fist forward for the punch while keeping your elbow down toward the floor for as long as possible. Make contact with the first two knuckles of your fist, making sure to keep your wrist straight. This increases the power of the punch, as well as your reach, and will help you deliver the punch safely.

2 Bring your hand and body back quickly to starting position, being careful to not let your hand drop when bringing it back toward your head. This protects your head and puts you in a position to throw follow-up punches.

Starting Position

Preferred Target Areas: solar plexus, groin

Striking Surface: first two knuckles (index and middle finger) of the fist

Starting Position: fighting stance

1 Extend your fist forward while bending at the waist and knees. Your body should "drop" as your punch develops. Drive the punch forward by pushing the ball of your back foot against the floor. Push off the floor to place more power in the punch. You may want to step slightly forward with your front foot to allow more space to bend down. Do not send the punch down while leaving your head up—this will leave your face open to a punch. If your fist goes low, your body needs to go lower.

Be sure to bring your hand back to your face as you rise after the punch.

Starting Position

A variation of a straight punch, the heel punch is a great alternative if you have long nails or injured knuckles, or are presented with a hard or bony target. Some people find it more comfortable to strike with the heel of the hand rather than the fist. Do not strike with your whole palm or hand, as the force of the punch will be dispersed along a wider surface area and will thus be weak.

Note: *The basic body movements here are the same as for the straight punch (page 46).*

Preferred Target Areas: chin, jaw, throat, nose, side and back of head

Striking Surface: heel of the palm

Starting Position: fighting stance

1 Driving with your legs and your core, send your right hand forward. Drive the strike forward and add power by pushing the ball of your back foot against the floor. Push off the floor to place more power in the punch. As your hips and shoulders rotate, extend your arm for the strike, keeping your elbow down toward the floor. Just before striking the target, flex your wrist backward, open your hand, and curl your fingers, making contact with only the heel of your palm (just where the wrist ends and the hand begins). Turn your hand slightly inward (to the thumb side) as you strike; this helps protect your hand and wrist.

Bring your hand and body back quickly to starting position, being careful to not let your hand drop when bringing it back toward your head. This protects your head and puts you in a position to throw follow-up punches. In most cases, this punch will have more power than the front hand (left, in this case) because the rear hip can pivot forward more powerfully.

Hammerfist Punches

Hammerfist punches can be thrown at most angles with formidable power. While the fist is made in the same way as for the straight punch (page 46), the striking surface for all hammerfist punches is the bottom of the fist. This makes hammerfist punches a "safe" alternative to traditional closed-fist punches, when the target surface is uncertain, because there's less risk of injury to the striker's hand. To further illustrate this point, you can beat on a door or wall relatively hard with this portion of your hand, without real risk of injury. Doing the same with your knuckles is certainly less desirable (and painful!). **Note:** The basic body movements for all hammerfist punches are the same as for straight punches.

Starting Position

Preferred Target Areas: chin, jaw, nose

Striking Surface: bottom of the fist (pinky side)

Starting Position: fighting stance

1 Raise your hand, moving it from chin height to about eyebrow height. While it's generally recommended to keep the hand forward of your ear, the emphasis should still be on big, powerful strikes.

2 As your fist comes down, rotate your shoulder and hip inward and forward and drive with your legs to generate maximum power.

Recoil your hand and body, returning to starting position.

Starting Position

Preferred Target Areas: back of head, back of neck, face (on a downed attacker)

Striking Surface: bottom of the fist (pinky side)

Starting Position: fighting stance

1 Raise your right hand, moving it from chin height to about eyebrow height. While it's generally recommended to keep the hand forward of your ear, the emphasis should still be on big, powerful strikes.

2 As your fist comes down, rotate your shoulder and hip inward and forward while dropping your weight at your knees to generate maximum power. Be careful not to bend at the waist as this will disturb your balance and take away from your power. Bend more at the knees so that your weight drops down. A small step out and forward with the lead leg may be necessary if you're too far from the target or just need the stability.

Recoil your hand and body, returning to starting position.

Starting Position

Preferred Target Areas: chin, jaw, nose, side of neck

Striking Surface: bottom of the fist (pinky side)

Starting Position: neutral position

1 Once the threat is recognized, tuck your chin and roll your shoulder up, allowing your elbow to lead the motion so you remain covered when turning into the fight. Send your hand sideways and upward with your elbow slightly bent.

2 As your hand moves toward the target, your hip and shoulder should rotate and your outside (or opposite-side) foot should pivot. Turning in to the fight is essential. Depending on your personal state of readiness and the target's location, you may strike and then step or step as you strike. *When early*, step with the same-side leg as you turn in to strike. *When late*, lead with your hand just after making contact, step, and turn in to the fight.

Variation: The hammerfist punch to the back is essentially the same as a hammerfist to the side, but with a greater turn.

Elbow Strikes

Elbow strikes are similar to hammerfist punches in that you can deliver them at almost any angle with power. However, unlike hammerfist punches, elbows are most effective at very close range (typically there is already contact between the defender and attacker). In order to create the most damage with the least effort, try to isolate the "tip" of the elbow, concentrating all of your power in a very small surface area. For virtually all elbow strikes, bring your hand to your shoulder, creating a sharp bend in the elbow.

Striking Surface for Elbow Strikes

The angles for elbow strikes are virtually endless. Here we present them in "spheres of attack" in order to illustrate how versatile these strikes are.

Starting Position

A strike forward, usually to the face or throat.

Preferred Target Areas: chin, jaw, nose, throat, sternum, side of head

Striking Surface: tip of elbow (slightly above or below the elbow is possible)

Starting Position: neutral position

1–2 Think about performing a straight punch with the point of your elbow, developing power by driving with your legs and rotating your hips.

Starting Position

A sideways strike against a threat from the side.

Preferred Target Areas: chin, jaw, nose, throat, sternum, side of head

Striking Surface: tip of elbow (slightly above or below the elbow is possible)

Starting Position: neutral position

1-2 Raise your elbow then punch outward (avoid a "flapping" motion). Make contact just above the tip of the elbow. Be sure to drive into the strike with your legs to give more weight and power.

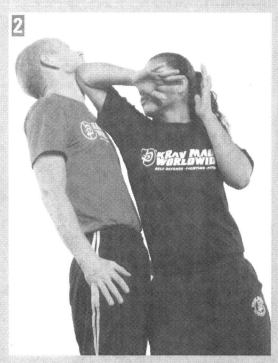

A strike backward.

Preferred Target Areas: chin, jaw, nose, throat, sternum, side of head

Striking Surface: tip of elbow (slightly above or below the elbow is possible)

Starting Position: neutral position

1–2 Once the threat is recognized, tuck your chin and bring your shoulder up, allowing your elbow to lead the motion so that you're covered when turning into the fight. As your elbow moves toward the target, your hip and shoulder should rotate and your outside foot should pivot (in the same manner as they do for hammerfist to the side, page 54). In order to travel through the target, drive with the opposite-side foot and hip.

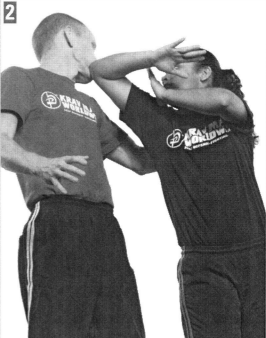

Starting Position

A strike to the ribs or stomach.

Preferred Target Areas: chin, jaw, solar plexus, back of head, back of neck

Striking Surface: tip of elbow (slightly above or below the elbow is possible)

Starting Position: neutral position

1–2 Snap your arm back into the attacker's body, shifting weight for more power. For any strike, you want to see the target; however, with a tight or close bearhug, the look may not be possible or needed.

Starting Position

A strike backward and upward to the throat or face.

Preferred Target Areas: chin, jaw, solar plexus, back of head, back of neck

Striking Surface: tip of elbow (slightly above or below the elbow is possible)

Starting Position: neutral position

1–2 To allow for the rising motion, you should tilt your shoulders forward, causing your elbow to rise.

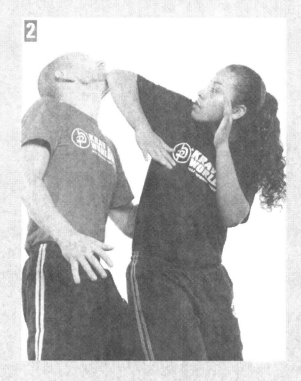

Starting Position

A strike forward and upward.

Preferred Target Areas: chin, jaw, solar plexus, back of head, back of neck

Striking Surface: tip of elbow (slightly above or below the elbow is possible)

Starting Position: neutral position

1–2 The striking surface is just below the tip of the elbow. Think of keeping your hand close to your head as you take your elbow up toward the ceiling. For additional power, drive from the ground with your legs in an upward motion through your hip and shoulder.

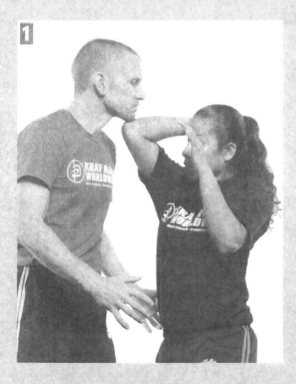

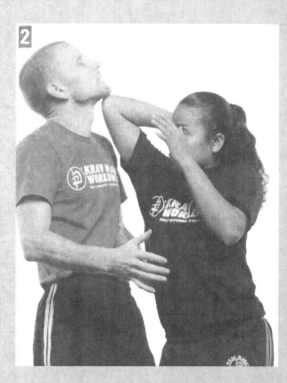

STRIKING BASICS **59**

Starting Position

A downward strike, similar to a downward hammerfist.

Preferred Target Areas: chin, jaw, solar plexus, back of head, back of neck

Striking Surface: tip of elbow (slightly above or below the elbow is possible)

Starting Position: neutral position

1–2 As with all strikes, you'll want to drive your weight behind every strike. In this case, changing your level by bending at the knees will help you to engage your body and maximize power. This strike works best if you're late in defending a frontal attack and are grabbed, like in a bearhug. In this case, the target area would be the base of the skull or back of the neck.

The forearm strike is an often-overlooked weapon that we feel should be incorporated into your arsenal. Again, we stress that you think in terms of utilizing as much of your body as a personal weapon as possible. The forearm is a very close-range weapon that's most effective when striking with the outer blade of the arm. This is a favorite technique of many football players since it allows you to really engage your entire body while using a body part that stays close to your core or power base.

Preferred Target Areas: chin, jaw, throat, sternum

Striking Surface: outer blade of forearm

Starting Position: fighting stance

1 The striking motion for a forearm is similar to that of the elbows in the horizontal sphere (see pages 54–56). However, instead of isolating a small surface area, you should think of smashing the target with the blade of your forearm. For all forearm strikes, bring your hand to your shoulder, creating a sharp bend in your elbow. To increase the power of the strike, you can burst forward with your entire body.

Starting Position

A headbutt can be a devastating weapon, both physically and psychologically, since it's outside of the proverbial box. Most people have an "idea" of what a fight or confrontation should look like. Headbutts don't fit inside that box. A headbutt must be performed at extremely close range. Be sure to keep your chin down and strike with the crown of your forehead against the soft tissue of your attacker's face.

Preferred Target Areas: chin, jaw, nose, sternum

Striking Surface: crown of head (preferably the hairline)

Starting Position: fighting stance

1 Keeping your neck stiff, your jaw tightly clenched, and your shoulders raised, drive your head forward using your legs and upper body. Strike with the top of your forehead, right at your hairline. Be sure to strike the attacker's face, anywhere below his eye line, with anything above your eye line. The objective is to strike with the hard part of your head to the soft part of the attacker's face.

While using your hands to assure your targeting is an advantage, it's important to know that you can and may need to deliver a headbutt without holding the head. In some bearhug positions, your hands may be caught and a headbutt is a good countering option.

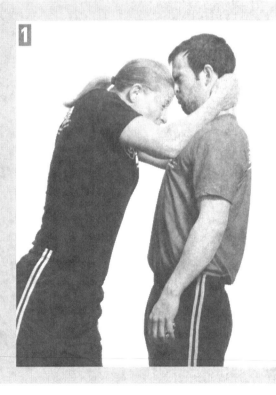

Note: While other headbutts are possible, for the purposes of this book we only show a headbutt to the front.

Kicks

Generally, legs are the longest personal weapons we have, so kicks are best used when the target is outside the reach of upper-body combatives, such as straight punches and hammerfists. Like other combatives, kicks are great tools when used in the proper context. They're range specific, though not all kicks are created equally with regard to range. For example, the rising front kick to the groin could be used from relatively close distances (striking with the upper shin) to farther away (striking with the instep). Offensive and defensive front kicks strike with the bottom of the foot, making them very long range relative to other combatives. Kicks generally allow the defender to do considerable damage while keeping the option of staying as far from the attacker as reasonably possible or necessary.

Kicks also tend to be the most powerful combatives, employing very large muscle groups and bones to inflict damage on would-be attackers. It's worth noting: Knees tend to be a close-range combative, much like elbows, but are also very forceful.

Starting Position

Preferred Target Areas: groin, leg, solar plexus, sternum, liver, kidney, face, head

Striking Surface: knee cap and the point just above kneecap (above the bent knee)

Starting Position: fighting stance

1 With your left hand, grab the attacker's right arm just above the elbow. With your right hand, grab his right shoulder and/or neck firmly by grabbing handfuls of skin. Keep your right elbow down, driving your forearm into his neck and/or collarbone. This will help give more control and reduce the chances of him grabbing you or taking you to the ground. (Reverse view also shown.)

2 Snatch your opponent's body forward and/or down while driving your right hip forward and your right knee forward and up, striking with the point just above your kneecap.

Be sure to recoil your entire leg back to the floor quickly so that the attacker has little opportunity to grab it.

Starting Position

Your legs are your longest personal weapons, and kicks are generally more powerful than punches. In Krav Maga we emphasize low kicks because they're more practical.

This kick is essentially the same as the Rising Front Kick to the Groin (page 66).

Preferred Target Areas: midsection of body or face (when attacker is doubled over)

Striking Surface: ball of the foot

Starting Position: fighting stance

1 Send your right hip forward and upward, allowing your slightly bent knee to follow.

2 As your hip comes forward, snap your foot, flexing your foot back to make contact with the ball of the foot. Note that your contact surface may change based on your target.

Starting Position

Preferred Target Areas: groin, face (when attacker is bent over)

Striking Surface: instep, shin

Starting Position: fighting stance

1 Send your right hip forward and upward, allowing your slightly bent knee to follow.

2 Snap your right foot out (point your toes away from you), driving up and through the target. You should make contact with any part of your leg just below the knee. The striking surface will be determined by how close the attacker is to you. Be sure to keep your hands up in front of your face while kicking.

Recoil by either putting your kicking foot down in front of you or bringing it back into a fighting stance.

Note: You can also kick with the forward leg. Being closer to the target allows for a faster kick, although it's not as strong.

Starting Position

Preferred Target Areas: solar plexus (anywhere from groin to navel is acceptable)

Striking Surface: ball of foot

Starting Position: fighting stance

1. Bring your right knee up toward your chest, with your toes pulled back toward your body, exposing the ball of the foot.

2. Punch your foot, leg, and hip straight out, not up. In order to penetrate the target and cause as much damage as possible, isolate the ball of your foot on impact.

Recoil. You should be able to make a strong kick and then plant your kicking foot as needed, either in front or recovering back to starting position.

Starting Position

The main purpose of a defensive front kick is to stop an advancing opponent or to increase space between the defender and attacker. For this reason, the entire bottom of the foot is used, since more surface area means the kick will push more than penetrate.

This kick is particularly effective if you're able to brace against a wall or car, allowing a stronger base. "Timing," or the ability to execute the kick at the proper distance and interval, is perhaps more critical with this kick than with others. If the kick is too early, you may miss and injure your knee. Too late and you won't be able to extend, forcing you to fall away on impact.

Preferred Target Areas: upper torso

Striking Surface: heel or entire sole of the foot

Starting Position: fighting stance

1 Bring your right knee up toward your chest, with your toes pulled back toward your body.

2 Send your foot forward, stomping with the entire foot. On impact, your knee should still have a slight bend to reduce your chance of injury and increase power. Be sure to drive your right hip into the kick, and also engage your base leg for more power.

Recoil (either forward or back) quickly.

Starting Position

A round kick is essentially a front kick on a horizontal plane.

Preferred Target Areas: the leg (just above or just below the knee), the thigh, the ribs, the head (if it's presented low)

Striking Surface: instep, shin

Starting Position: fighting stance

1–3 Make a front kick and, at the same time, roll your hip over while pivoting quickly on your base foot. When making contact, there should still be a slight bend in your knee. This allows the continuing motion to penetrate the target and also protects against hyperextension of the knee. To deliver the kick with power, be sure your base foot is "deeper" than the target, allowing your kicking leg to drive through. For more power you can step out at an angle (about 45°) and pivot simultaneously.

Recoil your foot back into a fighting stance.

continued on next page

continued from previous page

HELPFUL HINTS

- Pivoting is an important part of being able to deliver a strong round kick. You want to pivot on the ball of your foot, bringing your heel almost completely forward. This allows your hips to open up. Keep your weight in the ball of your base foot to allow your heel to move toward the target.
- The round kick can be given at various angles, depending on the target. It can be nearly vertical (to someone doubled over), diagonally upward (to the ribs), very horizontal (to the ribs or head), or even diagonally downward (to the thigh or knee).

Starting Position

This kick is for targets that are directly to your side.

Preferred Target Areas: midsection of the torso or knee

Striking Surface: heel

Starting Position: neutral position

1 Using the leg closest to the target, bring your knee and foot up in front of your body, keeping your ankle directly under your knee with your toes up.

2 Send the bottom of your heel toward the target while shifting your hips in the same direction. As your foot moves toward the target, pivot on your base foot (the foot still on the ground) so that the heel of your base foot points toward the target. Make contact with the bottom of your heel. There should be a slight bend in your knee when you make contact.

Recoil, making a sharp movement to bring your foot back toward you and down.

continued on next page

continued from previous page

HELPFUL HINTS

- For more power, drive your hips toward the target. For greater height, bend your body over the opposite hip.
- The target should be directly to your side but slightly out of your range.

Side Kick with an Advance or Advancing Side Kick Variation: Burst toward the target with a switch (back leg steps behind the kicking leg), simultaneously bringing your back leg toward the target while bringing your close leg up, knee chambered in front of your body.

Starting Position

Preferred Target Areas: midsection of the torso or groin

Striking Surface: heel

Starting Position: it's best to start with your kicking leg forward and lined up with the center of the target; as you build familiarity with the kick, it should be practiced from all positions

1–2 First, recognize the threat with a brief, natural glance over or to the side of your shoulder. Generally, you'll kick with the same-side leg that you look toward. Flex your kicking foot and send it backward toward the target, making contact with the heel. At the same time, thrust your hips backward into the line of the kick. In order to punch your hips into the target, you'll need to let your upper body bend forward a bit but still make sure to shift your hips back into the kick. Be careful not to look over your shoulder as it'll cause you to arch your back, which will interfere with the range and power of the kick.

Recoil to the starting position. When you first begin training this kick, you may end up with your back to the target. Once you feel comfortable with the kick, you should recoil and then turn on the base of your foot to face the aggressor and continue to attack, as necessary.

continued on next page

STRIKING BASICS **73**

continued from previous page

- With a closer target you can just send your kick from where you are.
- With a target at a slight distance you may need to take a step to reach with the kicking leg. In this situation, step back on one leg and kick with the other. The heel of the base leg should be pointed at the target for accuracy.
- When sending the kick, be sure to keep your knee and hip pointed toward the ground so that your leg travels straight back. If you allow your knee to rise and hips to open up, your kick may come from an angle instead of straight back.
- If you feel yourself falling forward (away from the target) when you kick, then your weight is in your shoulders—not in your hips. If you keep your weight in your shoulders, as you lower your body, you throw your center of gravity forward and fall that way. Instead, shift your weight into your hips and toward the target.
- You may also fall forward when the target is close and your kick is jammed. Being too close can prevent you from getting enough weight into the target.

Starting Position

This attack is generally made to an opponent who is behind you. This strike is useful as one possible counterattack against a bearhug from behind, especially when being lifted off the ground.

Preferred Target Areas: groin

Striking Surface: back of heel

Starting Position: neutral position

1. Raise your foot up sharply, striking with the heel—think of kicking yourself in the rear with your own heel. This will help you hit your target. Your knee should bend sharply, allowing a full range of motion. As much as possible, powerfully and suddenly lift your hip up with the help of your base leg for additional power.

1

Training Tip: Have your partner hold a kicking pad behind you and close to your body.

Variation: There may be times that chambering your knee is necessary. For example, when you're being lifted and your bodies are very close, you'll want to lift your knee slightly in front of your body to be sure your heel makes contact with the attacker's groin. If you only send your foot back, your calf will make contact with the groin and the foot with the butt. Think of kicking yourself in the butt with your heel from any position and you'll hit the intended target: the groin.

Starting Position

Preferred Target Areas: instep, ankle, groin (on downed attacker), head (on downed attacker)

Striking Surface: bottom of heel

Starting Position: neutral position

1 Bring your knee up toward your chest with your toes pulled back toward your body.

2 Send your foot down, stomping with the bottom of your heel. Keep your knee slightly bent upon impact to increase power and to reduce your chance of injury (such as hyperextending your knee). If targeting the instep, think of striking where the shoelaces are tied for maximum damage to the attacker.

Kicks from a Lying Position

Most of the kicks we've covered standing can be performed from a lying position. It's very possible during a violent encounter that you may end up on the ground, with a standing attacker. It's important to remain calm and continue the fight to get back up to a position of advantage. This is where you adapt your stance on the ground.

There are two basic positions you can adopt when on the ground: your back or your side. The way you fall could determine whether you're either on your back or side. While the back position keeps your head farther away, the side position offers easier mobility.

Back Position on the Ground

Lying on your back, lift your head and shoulders up off the ground with your chin tucked. Keep your hands up to protect your face. One foot is placed on the ground near your buttocks; the other knee is drawn up close to your chest with your foot flexed back. Your hips should be off the ground. Once this position is taken, only a small part of your back and one foot should be touching the ground.

Side Position on the Ground

Lie on one forearm, one hip, and one base leg—all on the same side. Keep your top hand up to protect your face. Your top leg is up with knee drawn back, ready to kick. If the attacker is farther away, you may rise onto your lower hand rather than your forearm, but ONLY if the attacker is farther away.

Starting Position

A front kick made in a stomping motion while on the ground can be especially useful when an attacker is directly in front of you.

Preferred Target Areas: (to a standing attacker) groin, midsection, head; (to an attacker leading with his head or on his knees) chest, head; a kick to the knee or shin is also possible (see variation)

Striking Surface: bottom of heel or entire foot

Starting Position: basic back position on the ground

1 As your kicking foot stomps outward, your base foot (the one still on the ground) drives into the ground to engage your hips and generate power. The use of the hips is most important. At the moment of impact, the only body parts touching the ground are the base foot and the shoulders/elbows.

Recoil immediately, bringing your knee back to your chest to prepare for another kick.

Variation: When kicking to the shin or knee, turn the foot outward slightly to broaden the kicking surface, giving the best chance to hit a target.

Starting Position

A round kick while on the ground can be especially useful when an attacker tries to make an end run around your defense or kicking leg. Essentially, this means your personal weapon (the kick) is no longer between you and the attacker, and the attacker has moved to a position where a stomping kick is no longer effective. As that happens, you should roll over and deliver a round kick using the leg farthest from the attacker.

Preferred Target Areas: knee, thigh, groin, head

Striking Surface: shin

Starting Position: basic back position on the ground

1 As the attacker moves around your defense, roll onto your hip and forearm in the direction of the attacker.

2 As the kick develops, lay the leg closest to the attacker on the ground as a base and deliver the round kick using your shin (just as in a regular round kick).

Recoil immediately, bringing your knee back to your chest to prepare for another kick.

continued on next page

continued from previous page

Target Variations: Based on your timing and your target, the kick may vary. If you have more time, you may lift your hip up off the ground for greater reach and power. Your target here could very well be the attacker's head if he's leaning forward. If you have less time and space to deliver the kick, you can make a slight scissoring motion to add power, shown below (this simulates the pivoting motion made during a standing round kick).

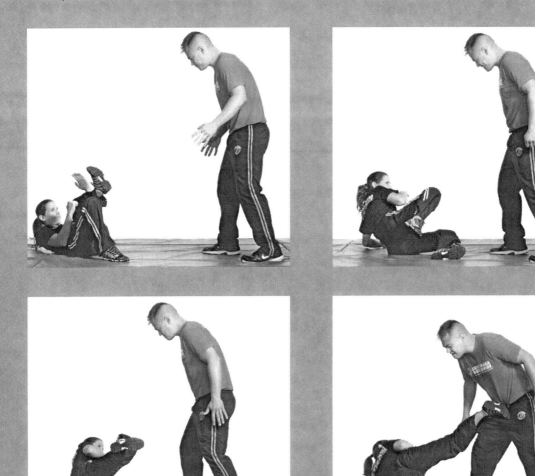

Starting Position

A side kick may be necessary after delivering a round kick, or if you end up on your side rather than your back.

Preferred Target Areas: knee, midsection, head

Striking Surface: heel or entire foot

Starting Position: basic side position on the ground

1 Send out your foot, extending your hip to generate power. Use your base hand (the one closest to the floor) for support and to give a push that helps generate power. Your other hand may also be used if the attacker is at a sufficient distance. Otherwise, that hand should be up in a defensive position. At the point of impact, your heel, knee, hip, and shoulder should all be in line to support the kick.

Recoil immediately, bringing your knee back to your chest to ready yourself to deliver another kick.

Defenses against Unarmed Attacks

Krav Maga, as a system, seeks to provide trainees with tools to survive a violent or potentially violent encounter. While there are several principles that drive "the Krav Maga approach," ultimately trainees should understand that fighting back aggressively is vital to survival. The previously discussed personal weapons are key to this "fight." Those faced with violence will need to strike back with anything and everything that's available, on their person and/or in the environment.

Krav Maga defines self-defense in simple terms: The attacker has committed himself to an attack, forcing the defender to respond with a defensive technique to eliminate the primary danger (either through sudden injury or incapacitation), thereby defeating the attack. Several main criteria should be used to examine and understand any self-defense technique in Krav Maga. The technique should:

- Be based on natural instincts/reactions.
- Be simple and useable by people of different strengths and body sizes.
- Address the immediate danger.
- Include a simultaneous (or nearly simultaneous) counterattack to neutralize further attacks.
- Be comprehensive enough to cover a wide variety of scenarios.

This section covers defenses against a variety of common attacks, including strikes, chokes, headlocks, and hair grabs.

Starting Position

This exercise serves as an introduction to outside defenses, which are defenses against attacks traveling from the outside inward, such as wild haymaker punches, hook punches, and knife attacks. There are seven basic positions. The 360° Defense is a reflexive exercise based on the body's instinctive reactions. It's made with the fingers extended since this is a more instinctive (reflexive) movement, which means it's quicker. The extended fingers also add a few inches to the defense.

Preferred Target Areas: attacker's wrist

Striking Surface: defender's wrist

Starting Position: For training purposes, first start in a neutral position with your hands up. Focus on the center of the attacker's chest and allow peripheral vision to see all attacks. If you turn your head to focus on one attack, you won't see an attack coming from the other side. Once you're comfortable with this, you can also train from a fighting stance.

Position 1: Raise your forearm above and slightly in front of your head to defend against an attack coming straight down.

Position 1

Note: To save time, you may move both hands at once. On the street, of course, the defense will be made with only one hand. After training with both hands, present the same movement using only one arm at a time. For the sake of reality, techniques are shown here using one hand.

Training Partner Note: Attackers should attack with very straight arms. While this is a fairly unlikely street attack, it makes an excellent training method both for developing the defense and peripheral vision. Attackers should begin slowly, one attack at a time, and increase speed as the defender improves.

Position 2: Raise your arm at an angle (like the roof of a house) to defend against an attack coming in at 45°.

Position 3: Send out your forearm perpendicular with the floor (if you use both arms, your arms will look like goalposts) to defend against an attack coming directly from the side.

Position 2

Position 3

continued on next page

continued from previous page

Position 4: Bring your elbow in tight to your body to defend against a rising attack to the ribs. Angle your forearm slightly outward and contract your ab muscles.

Position 5: Point your fingers down in a position opposite to position #3 to defend against a rising attack to the ribs.

Position 4

Position 5

Position 6: Lower your arm at an angle opposite of position #2. This is used to defend against a rising attack to the body. Note that you bend at the waist, NOT at the knees.

Position 7: Lower your forearm so that it's opposite of position #1. This is used to defend against a rising attack to the center of the body. Note that you bend at the waist, NOT at the knees.

Position 6

Position 7

continued on next page

continued from previous page

HELPFUL HINTS

- Always keep a 90° bend in the elbow.
- Defend using the blade of the arm.
- Bend at the waist. This will allow you to put your weight into the defense while keeping your body at a further distance from the attacker. Be careful to NOT bend at the knees. Why? Bending at the knees brings your body closer to the attacker. If the attacker has a knife, your bent knees may bring your body closer to the blade.
- Defend wrist to wrist. This guarantees a good defense. If you defend farther down the attacker's arm, you may allow the elbow to bend around the defense. If you defend too low on your own arm, the attacker's arm may slip below the defense. Additionally, when this movement is applied to a knife defense, the wrist-to-wrist motion guarantees a solid hold on the attacking arm.

"Defend and counterattack at the same time" is a basic principle of Krav Maga. The 360° Defense can easily be made with a simultaneous counterattack, such as a punch.

Preferred Target Areas: face

Striking Surface: fist

Position 2 (left) and Position 7 (right) with punch counterattack

Starting Position

An Inside Defense is made against straight punches to the face or throat. Unlike 360° Defenses, which are "stopping" defenses, Inside Defenses redirect or deflect an attack from its intended target—you.

Preferred Target Areas: back of the attacker's fist

Striking Surface: if the punch is to your face, make contact with the palm of your hand; if the punch is to your body, make contact with your forearm

Starting Position: fighting stance with hands up and slightly wider than the attacker's hands

1 As the right straight punch comes in, move your left hand forward and inward at a 45° angle, pushing with the center of your palm. The defense should be made against the back of the punching hand. The farther up on the arm that the initial contact occurs, the later the defense is made…and the closer the fist gets to your face before being redirected!

Training Partner Note: Attackers should begin at a slight distance so that they must advance to make a punch. This gives the defender a small comfort zone and teaches them that if anyone is inside that zone, they should be attacking rather than defending.

Note: Defenses are made with the same-side hand. No "cross blocking" (e.g., if the punch is made with the left hand, defend with your right).

2 Let your palm slide along the attacker's arm. At the same time, make a small head defense to your left and slightly forward to increase the margin for error. Generally speaking, the movement is slightly inward and to the side. Think of taking your head toward the crook of your arm, keeping your chin down and behind your shoulder. The forward motion also ensures that you keep your weight in the fight.

HELPFUL HINTS

- Small hand movements help the defender maintain a defense against a second attack or a feint. For instance, if the attacker fakes a left straight punch and throws a left hook instead, a big inside defense would move the hand too far away to recover and defend a hook. With a small movement, the defending hand is already there to defend the hook as well.
- If the defender keeps her hand near her face, she can only defend when the punch reaches her face. If she extends her hand diagonally forward, she goes out to meet the punch earlier and therefore farther away from her face.

Starting Position

Once you've mastered basic Inside Defenses and the 360° Defense, have the attacker deliver one punch at a time, but that attack can either be an outside attack, like for a 360° Defense, or a straight punch. You should begin to defend against either possibility. Be sure that your Inside Defense is made properly so that your hand is in a good position to defend outside attacks as well.

Starting Position: fighting stance

Training Partner Note: Attackers should begin at a slight distance so that they must advance to make a punch.

Attack

ATTACK In this attack, the attacker places both hands on the throat. The defender should train from a neutral position. Emphasis must be placed on the defender lifting the attacker's hands prior to sliding the attacker's hands outward.

IMMEDIATE DANGER *Thumbs on throat.* The primary danger in this attack is the potential of the thumbs crushing the windpipe. Without the thumbs, the attack is much less dangerous.

SECONDARY DANGER *Balance, headbutt.* In the attack and the subsequent defense, disruption of balance and headbutts (incidental or intentional) are possible. If the defense is performed properly, these peripheral dangers should be mitigated or removed altogether.

SOLUTION *Two-Hand Pluck.* The natural reaction to this attack is to bring the hands to where the danger or pain is. The plucking motion turns this instinct into a defense, which relies on explosiveness (speed) as opposed to strength. Since the pluck is derived from a natural movement, it's more likely to work under pressure. It'll also work regardless of whether the attacker's arms are bent or straight.

1 Create hooks with your hands by bringing your fingers and thumb together tightly and curling them slightly. Bring your hands up and over the attacker's hands, reaching deep inside at the point where the wrists and thumbs meet, plucking the attacker's hands up and out. This movement should be explosive from the beginning of the motion. Tuck your chin to guard against the potential of the attacker delivering an intentional or an inadvertent headbutt.

2 As the pluck continues parallel to your shoulders, pin the attacker's hands to your body. While this is not essential to the technique, it limits the attacker's weapons and will serve to prevent or delay secondary attacks. At about the same time, deliver a front kick to the groin.

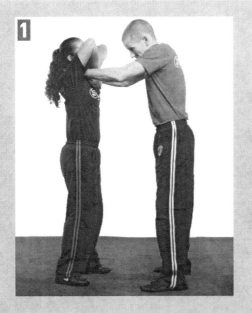

continued on next page

DEFENSES AGAINST UNARMED ATTACKS

continued from previous page

INITIAL COUNTERATTACK *Front kick to groin.* The front kick to the groin should be delivered as close to simultaneously to the pluck as possible. *Note:* Depending on the proximity of the attack, your knee may make contact first, but you should still throw the kick, since it may be difficult to assess the range in the moment.

NEUTRALIZING THE ATTACKER Typical follow-ups to the groin kick are knees, more front kicks, and/or hammerfists and elbow strikes to the face or the back of the head. Regardless of the combative used, focus on rendering the attacker unwilling or unable to continue the assault.

HELPFUL HINTS

- Explosive pluck, deep and at the wrist and thumb—think of the plucking action and direction ripping up and to a 90° angle against the attacker's hold. Plucking up and out is a strong action and, if performed explosively, the attacker cannot adjust in the moment.
- Trap attacking hands to body.
- Deliver simultaneous front kick to groin; follow up with aggressive combatives.
- Disengage when deemed safe.
- While it's important to counterattack quickly, it's necessary to eliminate the immediate danger first. In this particular case, it's possible that the kick would cause the attacker's grip to contract and increase the pressure on the choke if the pluck were not employed.

Safety in Training Note: Do not "punch" the hands into the defender's throat when training.

Neutralizing the attacker

Attack

ATTACK This attack happens to the defender's side, and the attacker places his hands on the throat and neck. The defender should train from a neutral position. The attacker should simulate a realistic attack, building in intensity as familiarity with the defense increases. One hand is positioned in front of the throat, while the other is placed on the back of the neck.

IMMEDIATE DANGER *Hands on neck and throat.* The primary danger in this attack is the pressure on the sides of the neck, which restricts the carotid arteries, and the potential crushing of the windpipe, depending on the position of the hand choking in front.

SECONDARY DANGER *Balance, follow-up attacks.* In the initial defense, it's possible to be exposed to an increased risk of tripping or being swept to the ground. The defender should also be aware of the potential for strikes from the attacker.

SOLUTION *One-Hand Pluck.*

1 Creating the same hook with your hand as in the front choke defense (page 93), this time using only the hand farthest from the attacker, reach up and beyond the attacker's hand.

2 In order be as explosive as possible, pluck where the wrist and thumb meet in a diagonal motion downward across your chest. To guard against an incidental headbutt, turn your head toward the attacker while simultaneously tucking your chin, exposing the top of your head to the attacker, not your face or the side of your head. As the pluck continues along your chest, pin the attacker's hand to your body. While this is not essential to the technique, it limits the attacker's weapons.

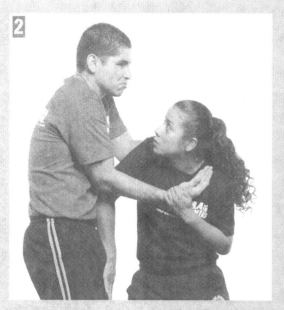

continued on next page

DEFENSES AGAINST UNARMED ATTACKS **95**

continued from previous page

INITIAL COUNTERATTACK *Strike to the groin.* As you pluck the attacker's hand from your throat, counterattack aggressively. One preferred strike is an open-hand slap to the attacker's groin. It's also possible to attack with an elbow immediately, instead of slapping the groin. In fact, if your hands happen to be up when the attack happens, this is probably a better option.

NEUTRALIZING THE ATTACKER Typical follow-ups to the groin strike are elbows to the face and head (hammerfists are also an option, if the attacker begins to move away from the strikes). Continue to strike while turning to face the attacker, which will allow you to transition to a more advantageous fighting position. Once this position is obtained, further counterattacks, such as knees and kicks, may be used more readily. Regardless of the strikes used, you must focus on rendering the attacker unwilling or unable to continue the assault.

HELPFUL HINTS

- Pluck explosively, diagonally across chest.
- Trap the plucked hand to body.
- Deliver simultaneous strikes to groin.
- Deliver aggressive, follow-up counterattacks while turning to engage attacker.
- Disengage when deemed safe.

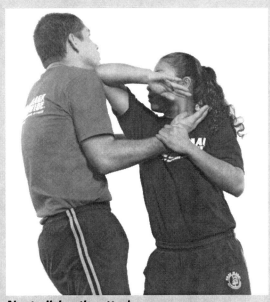

Neutralizing the attacker

Safety in Training Note: Do not "punch" the hands into the defender's neck when training, since this can cause a "whiplash" effect.

Attack

ATTACK This attack happens to the defender from behind, and the attacker places his hands on the neck and throat. The defender should train from a neutral position. The attacker should simulate a realistic attack, building in intensity as familiarity with the defense increases.

IMMEDIATE DANGER *Hands on neck and throat.* The primary danger in this attack is the pressure on the sides of the neck, which restricts the carotid arteries, and the potential crushing of the windpipe, depending on the position of the hand choking in front.

SECONDARY DANGER *Balance, follow-up attacks.* In the initial defense, it's possible to be exposed to an increased risk of tripping or being swept to the ground. The defender should also be aware of the potential for strikes from the attacker.

SOLUTION *Two-Hand Pluck.*

1–2 Send your hands as far back as you can, explosively plucking the attacker's wrist and thumb straight down. Shoot your raised elbows sharply down and to your sides. As your hands begin to move, tuck your chin and round your shoulders (you may find this happening instinctively). Step back diagonally with both feet to open up the groin, establish a good base, and move away from the attacker's free arm.

Safety in Training Note: Do not "punch" the hands into the defender's neck when training, since this can cause a "whiplash" effect.

continued on next page

DEFENSES AGAINST UNARMED ATTACKS **97**

continued from previous page

INITIAL COUNTERATTACK *Strike to the groin.* As you pluck the attacker's hands from your throat, counter-attack aggressively. One preferred strike is an open-hand slap to the attacker's groin.

NEUTRALIZING THE ATTACKER Typical follow-ups to the groin strike are elbow strikes to the body and face while turning to face the attacker, still controlling the attacker's outside hand. Depending on the attacker's reaction to these strikes, longer-range weapons such as hammerfists may be employed, and the hand may be released to continue with knees, kicks, and other counterattacks. Regardless of the strikes used, you must focus on rendering the attacker unwilling or unable to continue the assault.

HELPFUL HINTS

- Making the diagonal step mentioned above will also help reduce the chance of being tripped or swept.
- While it's preferred to use simultaneous counterattacks, it's not always possible. In this case, the attack is to the defender from behind, so strong counters are not available in tandem with the defense. The groin strike should still be made as soon as the immediate threat is addressed.
- While it's not a must to control the attacker's hand, it'll serve to prevent or delay secondary attacks, and it aids in keeping the attacker close for follow-up counters.
- If you don't continue the plucking motion to the groin, it's not really much of a problem: Simply transition immediately to elbows to the face, continuing to strike as you turn.
- From a technique standpoint, it makes no difference which side you move to when making the initial defense. However, there may be some tactical considerations that dictate moving one way or another (e.g., obstructions to one side, carrying of weapons, injuries, etc.).

Neutralizing the attacker

Attack ◄

ATTACK This attack happens to the defender's live side, and the attacker places both hands on the throat while pushing backward. The defender should train from a neutral position and should be pushed slightly off balance. The attacker should simulate a realistic attack, building in intensity as familiarity with the defense increases.

IMMEDIATE DANGER *Thumbs on throat, balance.* The primary danger in this attack is the potential of the thumbs crushing the windpipe, as well as being pushed off balance.

SECONDARY DANGER *Immediate environment.* Depending on the actual intent of the attack, the defender may be pushed into a wall, car, or other obstruction, further complicating the defense and increasing the danger. If the defense is performed early enough, this danger should be mitigated or removed altogether.

SOLUTION *Rotational Defense.* The natural reaction to this attack is for the arms to go up and for the defender to step back. Both of these motions are instinctual reactions designed to maintain balance, but the technique only requires one arm. This defense is very strong, and it'll certainly work against a "static" choke, or if there's no push. Krav Maga teaches the plucking defense first, since it's more instinctual and generally takes less time to learn.

1 As you step back with your left foot, stab your right arm straight up in the air, with the biceps and shoulder as close to your right ear as possible.

Safety in Training Note: Do not "punch" the hands into the defender's throat when training. Apply the choke, then the push, to minimize the risk of injury.

Training Tip: Allow the attacker to put you off balance before making the initial step. This will help to simulate a surprise attack. You may even start with your eyes closed to force you to defend "late."

continued on next page

DEFENSES AGAINST UNARMED ATTACKS

continued from previous page

2 Turn sharply to your left, creating pressure on the attacker's wrist and relieving pressure on your throat.

3 Drop your right elbow straight down for a downward vertical strike (elbow #7) in order to clear the hands, and trap the arms using your left hand.

Note: The defense can be made to either side, but for demonstrative purposes, sides have been designated.

Push against a Wall or Car Variation: All of the principles of "Choke from the Front with Push Backward" apply, but some points are different and must be emphasized to successfully defend in this scenario. This kind of choke must stress the fact that the defender may be driven both back into the wall and upward. Note that you can rotate in either direction to create the defense.

1 As the attack is performed, stab one arm up, pinning the attacker's wrist; drop the shoulder on the non-defending side down so that your body and neck stay against the wall.

2 With the shoulder down, you're now able to rotate in place, creating leverage on the attacker's wrist.

3–4 Drop the defending-side arm straight down for a downward vertical strike (elbow #7) in order to clear the hands, and trap the arms and immediately follow up with an elbow strike to the face.

Note: When you make the defense, DO NOT lean or rotate forward off of the wall. This will cause you to push your neck into the power of the choke.

INITIAL COUNTERATTACK *Horizontal Plane: Elbow #2 (page 55).* While not simultaneous to the defense, this elbow should immediately follow the clearing and trapping motions. Be sure to tuck your chin while delivering the elbow, and shift your weight into the counter.

NEUTRALIZING THE ATTACKER After the initial counterstrike, continue to strike with elbows and hammerfists to the head, while turning to face the attacker. Regardless of the combatives used, focus on rendering the attacker unwilling or unable to continue the assault.

HELPFUL HINTS

- When training, lean back to simulate being off balance.
- Arm stabs straight up to defend at the wrist.
- Turn sharply after stepping and stabbing. Remember, the sharp turn makes the defense, not the elbow. It's very important to stab the arm straight up and turn your body explosively. The technique does not rely on strength, but leverage.
- Put weight into the initial counter from the side.
- Use aggressive, follow-up combatives.
- Disengage when deemed safe.
- Train both sides after you've developed some familiarity with the defense. The defense works whether you step with the right foot and stab with the left or vice versa.

Attack

ATTACK This attack originates to the rear of the defender, and the attacker places both hands on the throat and neck while pushing forward. The defender should train from a neutral position and should be pushed slightly off balance. The attacker should simulate a realistic attack, building in intensity as familiarity with the defense increases.

IMMEDIATE DANGER *Neck, throat, balance.* The primary dangers in this attack are the potential of a whiplash effect to the neck, the fingers crushing the windpipe, and being pushed off balance.

SECONDARY DANGER *Immediate environment.* Depending on the actual intent of the attack, the defender may be pushed into a wall, car, or other obstruction, further complicating the defense and increasing the danger. If the defense is performed early enough, this danger should be mitigated or removed altogether.

SOLUTION *Rotational Defense.* The natural reaction to this attack is for the arms to go out and for the defender to step. Both of these motions are instinctual reactions designed to maintain balance, but the technique only requires one arm.

1–2 As you step forward with your right foot, stab your left arm straight forward, with your biceps and shoulder as close to your left ear as possible. Turn sharply to the left, creating pressure on the attacker's wrist and relieving pressure on your throat and neck. This turn should be greater than 90° in order to face the attacker. Also, be sure to turn in place, as opposed to moving your shoulder backward. The latter motion will create more resistance, making the defense harder to perform.

3 Continue to turn, stepping back with your left foot, establishing a strong base. Drop your left elbow down to clear and trap the attacker's hands.

INITIAL COUNTERATTACK *Punch.* While not simultaneous to the defense, this punch should immediately follow the clearing and trapping motions. In keeping with the description above, this would be a right punch to the attacker's face.

NEUTRALIZING THE ATTACKER After the initial counterstrike, continue to strike with knees. Regardless of the combatives used, focus on rendering the attacker unwilling or unable to continue the assault.

HELPFUL HINTS

- When training, lean forward to simulate being off balance.
- Arm stabs straight forward to defend at the wrist.
- Turn sharply after stepping and stabbing.
- Deliver aggressive follow-up combatives.
- Disengage when deemed safe.
- If your partner often goes right by you when you make the defense during training, it's very likely that you're doing nothing wrong. If the push is very strong, it's not only possible, but probable, that the attacker's momentum will carry him beyond you, which is why the step back is important.

Safety in Training Note: Do not "punch" the hands into the defender's neck when training. Apply the choke, then the push, to minimize the risk of injury.

Note: The defense can be made to either side, but for demonstrative purposes, sides have been designated.

continued on next page

continued from previous page

- Train both sides after you've developed some familiarity with the defense. The defense works whether you step with the right foot and stab with the left or vice versa.
- Krav Maga prefers to teach techniques that work for everyone. By wrapping the arms after you clear them, you give some measure of control to the attacker, and if the attacker is much larger or a better grappler, this can be very problematic. By simply pinning the hands with your elbow, you have the freedom of a quick release if needed.

Variation: Although often a safety issue in training, it's possible to strike with the elbow and/or hammerfist of the clearing arm. This is a faster counter, but it's difficult to train without actually striking your training partner.

Push against a Wall or Car Variation: All the principles of "Choke from Behind with Push Forward" apply, but some points are different and must be emphasized to successfully defend in this scenario.

1 As the attack is performed, stab one arm (the same arm you're facing) up, pinning the attacker's wrist. Drop the shoulder of the non-defending side down so that your body and neck stay against the wall. Unlike "Choke from the Front," you do NOT have the option of defending to either side. Your face will be turned to one side or the other, and you must pivot in the direction you're facing.

2 With the shoulder down, you're now able to rotate in place, creating leverage on the attack's wrist.

3–4 Drop the defending side arm straight down for a downward vertical strike (elbow #7) in order to clear the hands, and immediately follow up with a straight punch to the face. It's important to step in and establish a strong base as you're countering.

Attack

ATTACK This is the typical "schoolyard" headlock, where the attacker wraps his arm around your head and neck. The defender should train from a neutral position. The attacker should simulate a realistic attack, building in intensity as familiarity with the defense increases.

IMMEDIATE DANGER *Balance, pressure on the neck and throat.* The primary dangers in this attack are the potential of being taken to the ground and of the forearm restricting blood flow to the brain or crushing the windpipe.

SECONDARY DANGER *Punches.* The attacker's intent may be to hold the defender and punch to the face. If the defense is performed properly, this peripheral danger should be mitigated or removed altogether.

SOLUTION *High and Low Defense.* The natural reaction to this attack is to step to avoid falling or being taken to the ground. The arms are also likely to swing in order to aid in maintaining balance. Do not fight this natural inclination.

1–2 As the attack develops, step with it, turning your chin toward the attacker's hands, and tucking it in to provide a defense against punches and reduce the effects of a choke or strangulation. At the same time, your outside hand should swing low to the attacker's groin, and your inside hand should go high between your head and the attacker's head.

Safety in Training Note: Warm up your neck before training this attack and defense.

continued on next page

continued from previous page

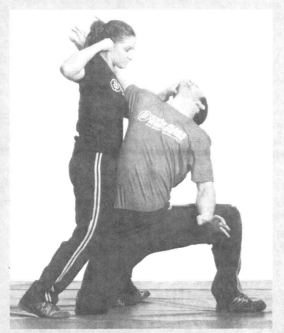 

Neutralizing the attacker

INITIAL COUNTERATTACK *Strike to Groin, Grab to Face.* The outside hand should slap or punch the groin as you're making the defense. The inside hand, placed between your head and the attacker's, should go to the attacker's face, with your thumb under the chin and index finger under the nose, avoiding the mouth.

NEUTRALIZING THE ATTACKER Lift the attacker's chin and drive the attacker's head straight down, while standing up with your legs and straightening your back. Continue to use hammerfists, palm heels, and punches to the face and throat while driving the attacker down toward the ground.

HELPFUL HINTS

- Go with the pull—do not resist it.
- Turn and tuck your chin to minimize the chance of being punched or choked.
- Simultaneously strike to groin and grab at face.
- Once the attacker's chin is up, drive your elbow (and the attacker's head) down.
- Do not follow the attacker to the ground while delivering counters.
- Deliver aggressive, follow-up combatives.
- Disengage when deemed safe.

Variations: There are other options if you cannot get at the attacker's face. ***If the attacker has hair***, make a grab at the hairline, pulling the head straight back and down, continuing with combatives. ***If the attacker has no hair***, it's possible to grab the muscle on the side of the attacker's neck and twist it to induce pain and create the needed leverage. In either case, you should still make the same motion with your elbow going down along the attacker's back.

Training Tip: It's very common for students to pull the elbow out instead of down. This will not allow for the kind of leverage and control needed to make the defense and deliver multiple counters. Think of turning the attacker's head back, making a "question mark" with your hand, arm, and elbow. After this motion, take your elbow straight down, keeping the attacker in one place, not rotating and pushing him away from you. Don't stop once you've created leverage on the neck and stood upright. Continue applying pressure to the neck and delivering combatives until the attacker is driven to the ground or taken off balance.

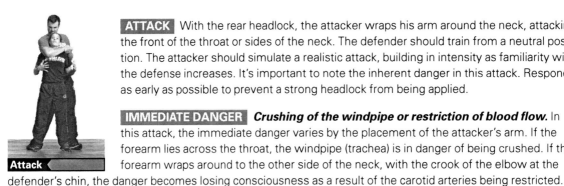

ATTACK With the rear headlock, the attacker wraps his arm around the neck, attacking the front of the throat or sides of the neck. The defender should train from a neutral position. The attacker should simulate a realistic attack, building in intensity as familiarity with the defense increases. It's important to note the inherent danger in this attack. Respond as early as possible to prevent a strong headlock from being applied.

IMMEDIATE DANGER *Crushing of the windpipe or restriction of blood flow.* In this attack, the immediate danger varies by the placement of the attacker's arm. If the forearm lies across the throat, the windpipe (trachea) is in danger of being crushed. If the forearm wraps around to the other side of the neck, with the crook of the elbow at the defender's chin, the danger becomes losing consciousness as a result of the carotid arteries being restricted.

SECONDARY DANGER *Balance.* In order to apply this headlock, it may be necessary or expedient for the attacker to pull the defender backward, compromising balance.

SOLUTION *Plucking.* The natural reaction to this attack is to bring the hands to where the danger or pain is. The plucking motion turns this instinct into a defense, which relies on explosiveness (speed) as opposed to strength. If possible, turn your chin toward the attacker's hands while tucking it down against your body.

1–2 Send both hands up and back toward the attacker's hands.

3 Pluck down explosively, 90° to the attack. If the attack is on the throat, this will mean along the chest. If the attack is on the sides of the neck, the pluck motion will be along the shoulder.

4–5 Continue to turn toward the opening created by the pluck and slide your head out immediately.

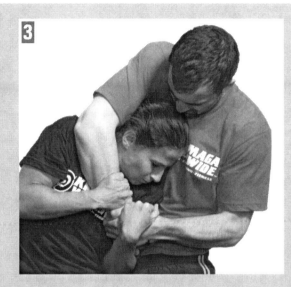

Safety in Training Note: Warm up your neck before training this attack and defense. Be careful not to apply too much pressure to the front of the throat. The attacker should also be aware of the potential for eye gouges.

Training Tip: While it's important to train from positions of disadvantage, this attack is extremely dangerous and difficult to defend if very late. You should place great emphasis on defending EARLY.

continued on next page

continued from previous page

INITIAL COUNTERATTACK *Shoulder strike.* Your inside shoulder should turn sharply into the attacker's body, creating more space in order to make it easier to remove your head from the hold.

NEUTRALIZING THE ATTACKER As soon as your head has been removed from the hold, immediately attack with knees, punches, hammerfists, or other available combatives.

HELPFUL HINTS

- Turn and tuck your chin as soon as possible.
- Pluck explosively, 90° to the attack.
- Send back the closed hand to the attack first, immediately followed by the second hand.
- After turning sharply with your shoulder, remove your head.
- Attack aggressively with whatever strikes are available.
- If you're not breaking the attacker's grip, it's possible that nothing is wrong with the defense. The plucking motion is designed to weaken the grip and eliminate pressure by creating space. It's not designed to break the grip, although it's attacking the attack's weakest point.
- In order to make the pluck as explosive as possible, think about sending the hands back, as if trying to strike the attacker's eyes, then plucking down. In most cases, going straight to the hands will not provide the momentum needed.
- If you can't get your head out after making the pluck, it's important to make sure that you're turning your chin and removing your head in such a way that it's narrower. Also, depending on the strength of the attacker, a strong and explosive shoulder turn should help to create additional space.

Defenses against Wrist Grabs and Arm Pulls

The context for arm grabs/wrist releases is based on the totality of the circumstances of the attack, not the attack itself. The true danger in being grabbed or pulled is that significant control is being exerted over your balance and mobility. You can be taken to the ground or pulled backward and be moved to a more secluded and isolated area, or be placed in a car and removed from the scene. Being moved to a more isolated area, in legal terms, constitutes a kidnapping, and is among the most dangerous situations you'll face. Statistically, when an assailant moves a victim to a more isolated environment, greater harm, such as rape, torture, and murder, is likely inflicted on the victim. Should you face this situation, every effort should be made to aggressively prevent it from occurring. Simply stated, you're fighting for your very existence—you're fighting for your life.

While all of these situations can potentially be dangerous, there is no immediate danger presented by having your wrist grabbed (unlike a choke, for example). The danger comes with the attacker's motive. By having a hold of your body, you can be controlled or taken off balance. Wrist releases are executed when the wrist grab itself does not present a true immediate threat. A simple release can serve to handle the situation while avoiding escalation. However, there are times when someone grabs your wrist and the circumstance calls for an aggressive counterattack. It's important to know how to free your hands to function in a fight. This is generally based on your personal assessment of the circumstance. Another context for wrist releases is from a ground-fighting position, where the attacker is attempting to control or pin the defender's hands. Being grabbed and pulled by the arm is another very common attack.

Note: A few principles to keep in mind for all wrist releases: The weakness in the attacker's grip is where the thumb and fingers meet or slightly overlap. When making a release, whenever possible, take your hand out toward the attacker's thumb.

ATTACK The attacker grabs your left wrist with his right hand, his thumb pointing up.

SOLUTION

1 With the blade of your wrist pointing toward the weakness in the hold (where the thumb and fingers meet), move your elbow forward and toward the attacker's elbow. At the same time, snap your wrist out of the hold, leading with the thinnest part of the wrist. It may be necessary to step forward to create the needed leverage and close the distance.

Attack

Note: If someone grabs one of your wrists, don't forget about your personal weapons. You have two legs and one hand free to strike the attacker if necessary.

2–3 Once the hand is released, you should bring both hands up and step away (preferably off to one side, as opposed to straight back) to create space and assess the situation.

Attack

ATTACK The attacker grabs your left wrist with his right hand, his thumb pointing down.

SOLUTION

1 Make a small circular motion outward toward the thumb, creating leverage to release the grip.

2 Finish the circular motion so that your hands come up but not in any sort of aggressive posture.

Step away (preferably off to one side, as opposed to straight back) to create space and assess the situation.

Attack

ATTACK The attacker grabs your right wrist with his right hand.

SOLUTION

1–2 Rotate your palm up and move your elbow forward, bending it in the direction of the attacker's elbow. In this position, it's unlikely that the elbows will touch, but you want to create leverage with this movement. At the same time, snap your wrist out of the hold, leading with the blade or thin part of the wrist. It may be necessary to step or lean forward to get your elbow close enough to the attacker's elbow to make the release. With a cross-side grab, a step forward will take your right side closer to the center of the attacker.

continued on next page

DEFENSES AGAINST UNARMED ATTACKS **115**

continued from previous page

3 Once the hand is released, bring both hands up and step away (preferably off to one side, as opposed to straight back) to create space, and assess the situation.

Attack

ATTACK The attacker grabs your left wrist with both of his hands.

SOLUTION

1–2 With your free hand, reach deep from underneath and in between the attacker's hands, and make the pluck close to his wrist. With only one hand remaining, this is now the same as Same-Side Grab (page 112).

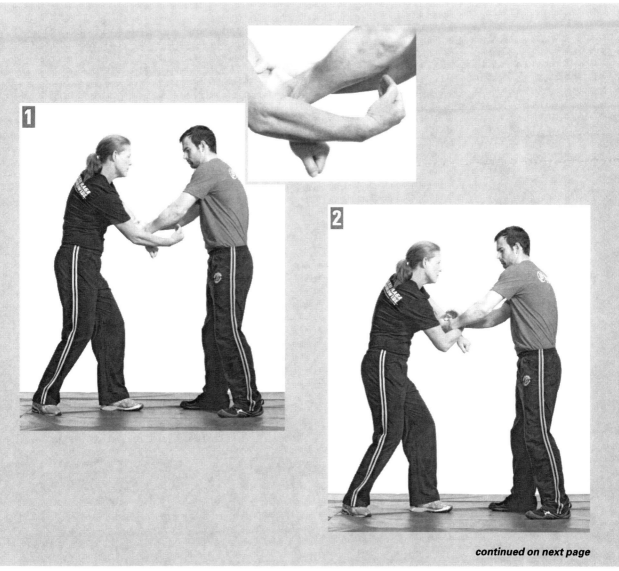

continued on next page

DEFENSES AGAINST UNARMED ATTACKS **117**

continued from previous page

3–4 At about the same time you're plucking, make a release from the hand still holding you by making sure the blade of your wrist is pointing toward the weakest part of the hold (where the thumb and fingers meet), moving your elbow forward, and bending it until it touches (or is very near) the attacker's elbow. At the same time, snap your wrist out of the hold, leading with the thin part of the wrist. If it's necessary to step forward to get close enough to make the release, do so with your right foot.

5 Once your hand is released, bring both hands up, step back to create space, and assess the situation.

Attack

ATTACK The attacker grabs both of your wrists and holds your hands down.

SOLUTION

1–2 Move your elbows toward the attacker's elbows. At the same time, snap your wrists out of his hold, leading with the thinnest part of your wrists.

3 Once your hands are released, bring both hands up, step away (preferably off to one side, as opposed to straight back) to create space, and assess the situation.

NOTE: Based on the circumstances of this grab, you may need to make an aggressive strike after you free your hands.

ATTACK The attacker grabs both of your wrists and holds your hands high.

SOLUTION

1-3 Make a circular motion "inward" with both hands (i.e., the left hand moves clockwise, the right hand moves counterclockwise). The small circular motions will create leverage on the thumbs. As you make the motions, lower your chin to your chest to protect against an incidental headbutt.

Attack

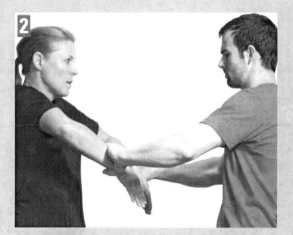

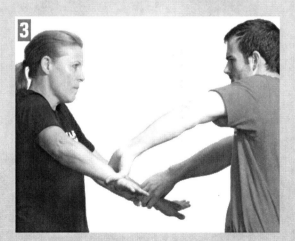

continued on next page

DEFENSES AGAINST UNARMED ATTACKS **121**

continued from previous page

4 Finish the circular motion so that your hands come up but not in any sort of aggressive posture. Step away (preferably off to one side, as opposed to straight back) to create space and assess the situation.

ATTACK The attacker grabs both of your wrists from behind and holds them behind your back.

SOLUTION

1–2 Turn your body in to your left and toward the attacker, allowing your elbows to bend but making sure to keep your elbows and hands close to your body. Bring your left hand in front of your body while rotating your palm upward, creating a chopping-type motion. Bring your other hand behind your back with the back of your hand facing your lower back.

Attack ◀

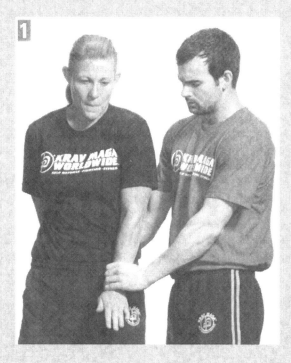

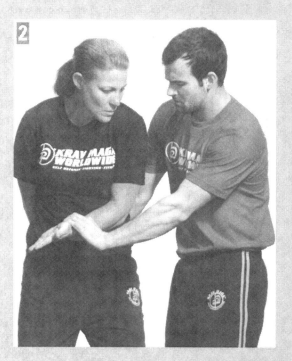

continued on next page

DEFENSES AGAINST UNARMED ATTACKS **123**

continued from previous page

3–4 With your left hand, make a wrist release followed by a quick hammerfist punch or elbow. Continue to counterattack until the threat is eliminated and you can escape.

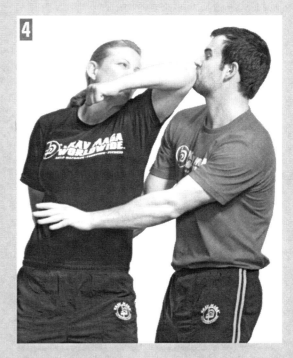

Attack

ATTACK The attacker grabs your arm and pulls you toward him.

SOLUTION

1 Burst in the direction of the pull, toward the attacker. If possible, burst toward the shoulder of the hand that's holding you. By doing so, you'll be less vulnerable to a punch from the attacker's free hand. With your free hand, counterattack as soon as possible. If your hand is low, strike the groin. If your hand is high, strike to the face, using a punch or elbow.

1

Attack

ATTACK The attacker grabs your arm from behind and pulls you toward him.

SOLUTION

1 Burst in the direction of the pull, toward the attacker. You may feel as if you're being "spun"—don't resist, burst! If possible, burst toward the shoulder of the hand that's holding you. By doing so, you'll be less vulnerable to a punch from the attacker's free hand.

2 With your free hand, counterattack as soon as possible. If your hand is low, strike the groin. If your hand is high, strike to the face, using a punch or elbow.

Attack

ATTACK The attacker approaches you from behind and uses his left hand to grab your left upper arm or the shoulder area of your body; he cups his right hand over your mouth, or over both your mouth and nose. You'll be unable to yell for help or to attract attention.

IMMEDIATE DANGER **Restricted breathing, increased panic, loss of balance.** If the attacker's hand covers both your mouth and nose, it'll be more difficult for you to breathe. Interrupting your ability to breathe causes a multitude of additional issues: It'll be difficult to fight back strongly and effectively when the body is depleted of oxygen. Once breathing is restricted, panic sets in. Once panic sets in, tactical decision making and the ability to perform physically deteriorate.

SOLUTION

1 Raise your right hand above the level of the attacker's arm covering your mouth and nose. Try to keep your hand movement hidden from the attacker's line of sight. Keep your hand cupped and your arm close to your body.

continued on next page

DEFENSES AGAINST UNARMED ATTACKS **127**

continued from previous page

2–3 Pluck downward explosively at the wrist. The pluck should be at a 90° angle relative to the position of the wrist covering your face. This will remove the attacker's hand from your face. As you pluck, move diagonally back and to the same side as your plucking hand (to the right of the attacker in this scenario). You'll now be able to breathe and yell to attract attention, but don't stop in this position. You must make a seamless transition from defense to counterattacking in order to stun and inflict damage on your attacker. Control the hand that you've removed from your face so that it can't be used against you.

4 Attack aggressively by stomping on the instep of the attacker's foot using the heel of your foot. Turn in, keeping your chin tucked and protected in order to face the attacker while delivering a barrage of attacks, such as punches, eye gouges, elbows, and knees. When able to do so, flee the scene.

Attack

ATTACK The attacker grabs your hair from the front.

IMMEDIATE DANGER **This is a hold.** All dangers are secondary.

SECONDARY DANGER **Being punched, kneed, headlocked, or taken to the ground.**

SOLUTION

1–2 Bring both hands up and slam them sharply down over the attacker's hand. This punches his knuckles against your skull, causing him pain. Be sure to keep your elbows in so that your forearms protect your face against a punch (which is most likely).

continued on next page

DEFENSES AGAINST UNARMED ATTACKS **129**

continued from previous page

3 Immediately bend forward sharply at the waist (think of taking a bow); this causes immediate pressure against his wrist. Do not send your hips backward. Allowing your hips to push backward relieves this pressure.

4 As the attacker drops down, quickly move backward to stretch out his body.

5 Immediately follow up with front kicks to the face.

Attack

ATTACK The attacker grabs your hair from the side and pulls you toward him.

IMMEDIATE DANGER **Balance being compromised.**

SECONDARY DANGER **Being punched, kneed, headlocked, or taken to the ground.**

SOLUTION

1 Burst in the direction of the pull—do not resist. If possible, burst in toward the shoulder of the hand that's holding your hair. This limits your vulnerability to a punch from the attacker's free hand. As you burst in, use your close hand to reach up and grab the hand holding your hair. This is an instinctive movement that often helps limit the attacker's control. However, you won't completely regain control of your body movement unless you burst in.

2 With your free hand, counterattack. From an unprepared state, with hands down, the fastest and simplest counterattack will be to the groin. However, if your hands are up for any reason, you may just as easily counterattack to the face with a punch or even an elbow, depending on the distance.

Variation: If you feel yourself being pulled down, make a 360° Defense against the knee strike that is most likely coming. See Hair Grab from the Front or Side (Impending Knee Strike) on page 132.

DEFENSES AGAINST UNARMED ATTACKS **131**

Attack

This technique works for either a front or side grab.

ATTACK The attacker pulls you down by your hair, likely in an attempt to make a knee strike to your face.

IMMEDIATE DANGER **Being kneed in the head or face.**

SECONDARY DANGER **Continued attacks.**

SOLUTION

1 As your upper body is pulled down, make 360° Defense #7 with the closest arm against the rising thigh. At the same time, strike to the groin with your free hand.

2 Immediately follow up with a counterattack. Note that if you end up "cross-blocking" (e.g., you defend with your left hand against the attacker's left knee), your counterattack will be delayed. Make it as soon as possible after the defense. Continue driving forward with your body to relieve any remaining pressure or control from the hair grab. If possible, straighten up to avoid any more knee strikes to the face, and continue with counters.

Note: If the hair grab is from the front and no more knee strikes are impending, you can continue with regular Hair Grab from the Front (page 131).

Attack

ATTACK The attacker either comes from the side but grabs the hair on the back of your head, or reaches around to the other side. The attacker could also come from the back and grab the hair on the back of your head.

IMMEDIATE DANGER Balance being compromised.

SECONDARY DANGER Being punched, kneed, headlocked, or taken to the ground.

SOLUTION

1 Burst in the direction of the pull—don't resist it. If possible, try to burst in toward the shoulder of the hand that has grabbed you. This limits your vulnerability to a punch from the attacker's free hand. If you feel yourself "spin" around, go with this motion.

2 As you're spun around, make a 360° Defense (if necessary) with the closest hand. If there's no knee strike, make a counterattack to the groin with the closest hand.

Defenses against Bearhugs

Bearhugs represent a common type of attack, especially against women. Bearhugs may be a part of many dangerous scenarios, including being carried into a secluded area, being dumped on the ground, or being held for additional attackers. While all of these situations are dangerous, there's no immediate danger presented by the bearhug itself. Unlike chokes, bearhugs do not cause immediate damage, as the attacker's intention with the bearhug is the problem. This is important because with no immediate danger to address, Krav Maga's response is to counterattack immediately.

The techniques detailed in the following pages assume that either there's some delay in the attacker taking you to the ground (caused by you or the attacker's method) or that his intention is to hold you or take you somewhere, rather than put you on the ground immediately. Assuming you're surprised, if the attacker's intention is to take you to the ground, it's very likely that you're going to the ground and will fight from there.

Attack

ATTACK The attacker wraps his arms over your arms and around your body from the front.

SOLUTION

1 As the bearhug is applied, "base out" by punching your hips back to drop your weight down, while separating your feet into a wide stance. Strike to the groin with your hands or knee if you need to create space first. Send the heels of your palms to the attacker's hips to prevent him from closing the space you created.

2 Deliver knees and/or front kicks immediately to the groin or midsection. As soon as enough space is created, bring a hand up and lay a forearm across the attacker's neck for control (see Knee Strike on page 64 for details on this position). Continue to strike the attacker and escape as soon as the threat is eliminated.

Attack

ATTACK The attacker wraps his arms around your body but under your arms from the front.

SOLUTION

1 As the bearhug is applied, "base out" by punching your hips back to drop your weight down, while separating your feet into a wide stance. At the same time, send the heels of your palms to the attacker's hips while reaching around his arms.

2 Deliver knees and/or front kicks immediately to the groin or midsection. As soon as enough space is created, bring a hand up and lay a forearm across the attacker's neck for control (see Knee Strike on page 64 for details on this position). Continue to strike the attacker and escape as soon as the threat is eliminated.

Attack

ATTACK The attacker wraps his arms around your body but under your arms from the front. However, you've managed to "space and base" enough to use other tools. As the attacker squeezes you in, his head turns to one side against your chest (for illustrative purposes, we'll designate this as the right side).

SOLUTION

1 With your left arm, reach around the attacker's head and grab his hair at the temple. If the attacker has no hair, reach slightly farther and grab along the nose ridge while pressing into the eyes.

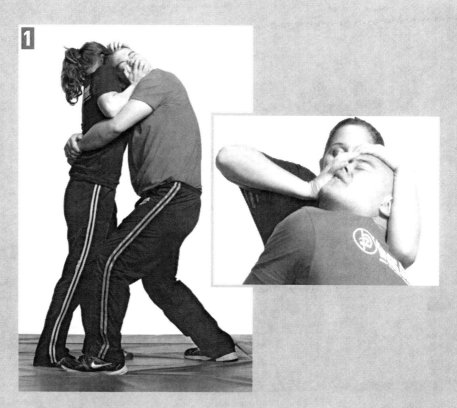

continued on next page

DEFENSES AGAINST UNARMED ATTACKS **137**

2–3 Twist the attacker's face away from your body, forcing the side of his head away from you. Use your right hand to aid this motion by striking the heel of the palm against his chin and pushing. As you peel the attacker away, step back with your left foot, driving the attacker toward the ground.

If he goes to the ground, attack with kicks and stomps. If space is created but he's still upright, counter with punches.

ATTACK The attacker wraps his arms around your body but under your arms from the front. However, you've managed to "space and base" enough to use other tools. As the attacker squeezes you in, the front of his face turns toward your body.

SOLUTION

1–2 Gouge his eyes with your thumbs, causing his head to tilt back and creating the space you need to strike the attacker and escape.

Attack ◄

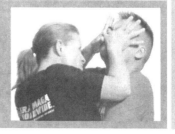

Variation: It's also possible to use the webbing between your thumb and finger under his nose to drive his chin up.

Attack

ATTACK The attacker wraps his arms over your arms and around your body from the front and lifts you off the ground.

SOLUTION

1–2 Counterattack immediately with knees to the groin and/or solar plexus. If you land a strong and solid knee, the attacker may drop you quickly. Be ready to get your feet under you fast!

3 Once your feet are back on the ground, continue to counter. Escape as soon as the threat is eliminated.

Variation: If your hands are free, it's also possible to grab his hair, attack his eyes, leverage his chin, and/or counter-attack with strikes to the face or throat.

Attack

ATTACK The attacker wraps his arms over your arms and around your body from behind.

SOLUTION

1–2 When the grab is made, immediately drop your weight to make yourself more difficult to lift. Strike at the groin and midsection to create space. The attacks should cause damage and also create movement and space, making you more difficult to hold.

3 As soon as enough space is created, turn to face the attacker and continue counterattacking, escaping as soon as the threat is eliminated.

Variation: Additional initial counterattacks may include stomps and short back kicks to the groin.

Attack

ATTACK The attacker wraps his arms around your body but under your arms from behind. The attacker's head is not pressed against your back.

SOLUTION

1 When the grab is made, immediately drop your weight to make yourself more difficult to lift.

2–3 Send horizontal elbow strikes backward to his face in a left-right or right-left combination.

4 If the elbows create space, turn and continue with strikes. If the elbows don't create space, continue with additional strikes, including stomps to the feet and short back kicks to the groin.

Attack

ATTACK The attacker wraps his arms around your body but under your arms from behind. The attacker also tucks his head against your back, limiting your ability to make counterattacks with your elbows.

SOLUTION

1 As the bearhug is initiated, immediately drop your weight to make yourself difficult to lift.

2 Send elbow strikes to the attacker's head. However, if the elbows aren't making contact, quickly strike the back of the attacker's hand with your knuckles to loosen his grip.

3–4 Slide your hands along his forearms until you find a finger (usually his index finger). Starting at the tip of the finger, peel the finger up and away.

5–6 As you loosen the finger, grab it with your opposite hand (i.e., if your left hand is squeezing the knuckles, grab the finger with your right) so that the meaty part of your hand is near the base of the finger and the thumb side of your hand is at the tip. Think of pushing the finger rather than pulling it, and, with your left hand, grab and squeeze the attacker's hand to isolate the finger. Press the finger down into its socket, then push back toward the attacker's hand. This releases the bearhug.

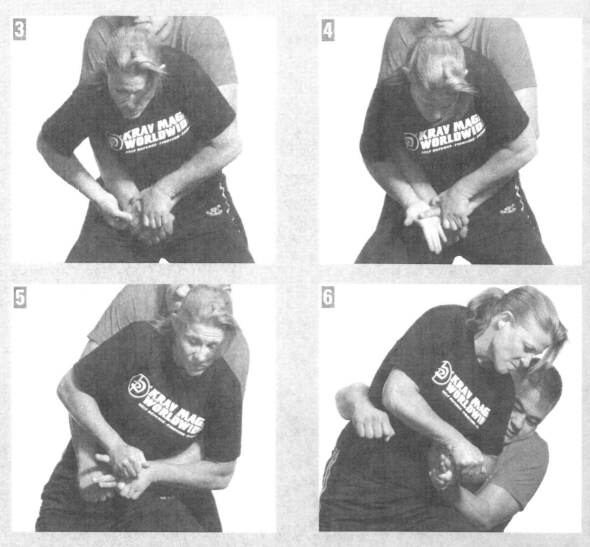

continued on next page

continued from previous page

7–8 Pivoting on your foot, step out, keeping pressure on the finger.

Kick to the groin or face and continue counterattacking, escaping as soon as the threat is eliminated.

Attack

ATTACK The attacker wraps his arms around your body from behind and lifts you off the ground. The defense is the same whether your arms are free or caught.

SOLUTION

1–2 Counterattack immediately with short back kicks to the groin and wrap your free leg around the attacker's leg and straighten it. *Note:* If you land a strong and solid kick, the attacker may drop you quickly. Be ready to get your feet under you fast! Additionally, while the wrap is important, do NOT wait until after you've wrapped to make the kick.

Once your feet are back on the ground, continue to strike the attacker and escape as soon as the threat is eliminated.

Groundfighting

Simply stated, all things being equal (and that's never the case), it's preferable to avoid the ground in a self-defense situation. That said, it's important to recognize that self-defense situations are dynamic and, by definition, the defender has been caught off guard and is reacting to an attack. Therefore, it's not always possible to avoid the ground. Furthermore, most sexual assaults are going to be committed on the ground (the "ground" being used as a universal term for defending while your body is horizontal, not vertical).

In the event that a defender is in a "groundfighting" situation, Krav Maga's approach is to use positions and techniques that are designed to get the defender back to her feet as soon as possible. Understand that the "goals" of groundfighting, as distinguished from grappling, are to use groundfighting skills to escape from a grappling scenario. In other words, the defender wants to get away and escape as soon as possible and not stay in an effort to subdue, submit, or control the attacker.

Basic Positions on the Ground

There are many positions that a defender could be exposed to on the ground. However, for the purposes of this book, we'll focus on the two most common, particularly for women. ***Note:*** We will not address these positions from an "offensive" perspective in this book.

The **guard** is a common position for a sexual assault situation. The attacker is between the defender's legs and close to the body. From a defensive standpoint, there are two basic options when using the guard. In order to best control your attacker, you should cross your ankles behind his back, encircling him with your legs. This is referred to as *closed guard*. Generally, for self-defense, this is not preferred since it limits your options and your ability to get back to your feet. This is not always the case, but when using a closed guard in this context, it's important to remember not to stay there for long.

Closed guard

Conversely, an *open guard* involves keeping your feet apart and legs "open." This position is generally preferred in a self-defense situation since it offers you more options to attack and escape quickly.

The **full mount** is a position in which the attacker sits on top of the defender, straddling the defender's body. This is a very dominant and dangerous position. As such, it's important to be very active from the bottom and do damage through strikes, chokes, etc., making it difficult for the attacker to maintain his balance.

Open guard

Full mount

Attack

ATTACK The attacker has you in full mount.

IMMEDIATE DANGER **strikes to the head and face**

SECONDARY DANGER **second attacker, head hitting the ground**

SOLUTION

1 Bring your elbows in close to your body, keeping your hands up and covering your face. Tuck your chin and keep your head off of the ground. Bring your feet as close to your body as you can. Do your best to keep your attacker over your hips to maximize your ability to disrupt his balance. Do not let the attacker move up to your chest.

Modification: If the attacker manages to maneuver higher on your body, work your elbows into his thighs while wriggling your upper body away so that he ends up back over your hips.

2–3 Buck your hips up explosively, forcing the attacker to struggle to maintain balance. If necessary, use your arms much like the punch defenses (Inside or 360° Defenses) previously discussed from standing, but do not rely on this. You MUST be very active from the bottom to avoid being struck hard. *Note:* "Bucking" only provides a temporary solution for the punches. Bucking alone only buys you time and an opportunity to execute an escape.

HELPFUL HINTS

In order to create the most powerful bucking movement, be sure that the heels of your feet are as close to your butt as possible. Drive through with your feet to lift your hips as high as your knees. At this point only your feet and shoulders should be touching the floor. You should practice this without an attacker to get a feel for the movement.

Attack

ATTACK The attacker has you in full mount.

IMMEDIATE DANGER **strikes to the head and face, being choked**

SECONDARY DANGER **second attacker, head hitting the ground**

SOLUTION

1 Buck your hips, breaking your attacker's balance and forcing him to "base out" or place a hand or hands on the ground.

Note: It may take several attempts at bucking and/ or trapping to achieve success. Also, while we describe two methods of trapping here, others are possible, including (but not limited to) grabbing clothing or grabbing one arm with both of yours.

2-3 Trap one of his based-out arms with one of yours by either reaching over or under the attacker's arm. While trapping the arm, trap the attacker's leg/foot on the same side as the arm. *Note:* Reaching over the arm usually makes for a better hold but may take longer. Trapping the arm above the elbow gives you better control of the arm.

4-5 Explosively buck your hips again, driving up toward your head and over your shoulder on the "trapped" side.

continued on next page

continued from previous page

6–7 Immediately strike to the attacker's head with elbows, hammerfists, palm strikes, etc., as you "posture up," striking down the attacker's center. Get up as soon as possible.

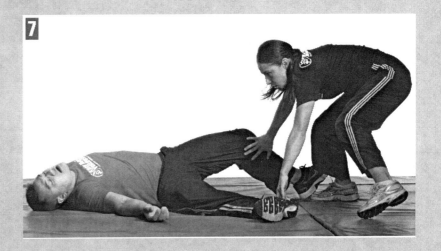

Attack

ATTACK The attacker has you in full mount. The defense may be performed to either side but, for demonstration purposes, we first make it to the left.

IMMEDIATE DANGER **being struck in the head and face, being choked**

SECONDARY DANGER **second attacker, head hitting the ground**

SOLUTION

1 Get on your left hip (an initial buck may be helpful here) and wedge your left elbow between your body and the attacker's right knee in order to create and maintain space.

2 Straighten your left leg and drop it flat to the floor. Your right leg should be bent, with the bottom of your foot firmly on the floor.

continued on next page

GROUNDFIGHTING **157**

continued from previous page

3 Using this foot and leg, push your hips up and out toward your right. Use your right hand to push the attacker's knee away while simultaneously pushing your body up and away from the attacker (remember, it's generally easier to move you than someone else).

4 Once you've created space between you and the attacker's right knee, bend your left knee, taking it toward your left elbow, and slide that leg up and out. This leg must remain flat on the floor in order to slide it out or under the attacker's leg.

5 Once your left leg is successfully out, wrap it around the attacker's leg on that same side and then switch to your right hip.

Repeat the same set of movements to the right side. If enough space was created during this movement, kick off and look to escape to your feet. Otherwise, wrap both legs around the attacker's body until you're able to maneuver to a more advantageous position.

Attack

ATTACK The attacker has you in full mount and has both hands on your throat.

IMMEDIATE DANGER being choked

SECONDARY DANGER head hitting the ground, being punched, additional attackers

SOLUTION

1-2 Pluck his hands from your throat and trap them to your shoulders, much like the basic defense from standing (page 93). At the same time, trap one of his legs with your foot (assuming you trapped both hands, it doesn't matter which leg you trap).

continued on next page

GROUNDFIGHTING **159**

continued from previous page

3 Explosively buck your hips, driving up toward your head and over your shoulder on the "trapped" side. This should happen at the same time as the pluck.

4 Continuing to push the ground with both feet, roll your hips over toward the trapped side.

5 Immediately strike to the attacker's head with elbows, hammerfists, palm strikes, etc., as you "posture up," striking down the attacker's center.

Get up as soon as possible (see "Escaping the Guard" on page 161 for more information).

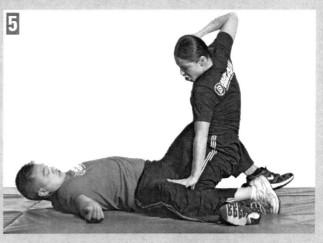

While there are plenty of guard escapes, generally the simplest approach is preferred.

ATTACK The attacker holds you in closed guard.

IMMEDIATE DANGER being punched, choked, and/or sexually assaulted

SECONDARY DANGER head hitting the ground, additional attackers

SOLUTION

1–2 When put in the guard, you'll want to use strikes or other combatives to create distance, while "posturing up" to avoid having your head grabbed.

Modification: If the attacker brings his knees in to protect his groin, put your hands on his legs (inside his knees) to prevent him from kicking you or reestablishing the guard.

continued on next page

continued from previous page

3 Keep your back straight while striking the groin.

4–5 With a good groin strike, it's likely the attacker will bring his knees in to protect his groin, creating an open guard. Put your hands on his legs (inside his knees) to prevent him from kicking you or reestablishing the guard. While maintaining your weight in your legs, stand up and move away. Be careful not to commit your weight on the attacker's knees to help yourself up.

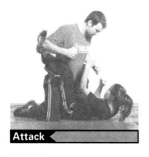

ATTACK The attacker is in your guard. The technique may be performed to either side but, for demonstration purposes, the defense is first made to the left.

IMMEDIATE DANGER being punched, choked, and/or sexually assaulted

SECONDARY DANGER head hitting the ground, additional attackers

SOLUTION

Attack

1 Shift to your left hip, bringing your right shin in against his body. Keep your hands up to protect against strikes.

continued on next page

continued from previous page

2–3 Put your left heel on his hip to create and maintain space. Use your right foot to kick to his face or chest.

4 Get up and move away as soon as possible. ***Note:*** Multiple kicks may be required, but it's important to get to your feet as quickly as you can.

Using Everyday Objects as
Defensive Weapons

When an assailant attempts to harm you, inflict serious bodily injury, or do anything to place your life in danger, you must be trained to fight back aggressively, without limitation and without rules. Street fighting is a no-holds-barred battle to survive. Do whatever it takes to overcome a violent encounter, even if that means to arm yourself with everyday objects available to you. Using an everyday object to shield yourself from harm and/or inflict damage on your assailant is a tactically sound way to successfully thwart, intimidate, overcome, and defeat your attacker.

Be prepared for victory well in advance of when danger presents itself. This section presents common objects that can be used to your benefit. In order to survive, your mindset should be open to include the use of everyday objects available in your environment both as defensive and offensive weapons. There are various types or categories of objects in almost any environment. Know what these objects are and how to tactically acquire and use them. In many cases, everyday objects can be used to improve your odds of surviving an unarmed or armed assailant.

In order to access a common object in the environment, you have to be aware of your surroundings. You must be able to quickly identify those objects that can be of use to you. Awareness is not merely limited to noticing other people near you nor being aware of routes of escape so that you can flee the zone of danger. An essential element of readiness is to possess a heightened state of awareness that necessarily includes the ability to recognize and identify common objects present in the area where the confrontation occurs.

But how do you train yourself to identify useful objects? It all begins with knowing which objects can be helpful to you. This section will specify many valuable objects for your use. The list, of course, is endless. The number of items that you can identify and access is only limited by your ability to envision the potential of those items as tools to defend against and to attack your assailant.

Each day push yourself to develop a higher state of awareness as to the common objects in your environment. Whether you sit at home or work, visit a market/doctor's office/restaurant, or walk down a street, critically analyze the different areas and the overall environment to see what object is available to you. Count all of the common objects that you could use to defend yourself and to effectively disable and stop your attacker. Consider the type of weapon it is. What are its strengths and weaknesses? Improve your awareness of what you can instantly access should a threat to your safety occur.

HELPFUL HINTS

- Use strong objects against weak objects/points on the attacker.
- Learn to block the attack at a 90° angle.
- Learn to redirect the line of the attack.
- Strike powerfully and often.
- Strike to the most vulnerable areas of the attacker's body.
- Swing or stab using all angles (upward, downward, horizontally to the left and to the right, forehand, backhand, and straight) to attack your assailant.
- Train to defend against attacks directed at you from every angle and to different levels on your body, and involving variations in timing and speed.
- Develop the ability to defend and attack in a sphere-like zone.

Your Level of Readiness to Access Objects

Not all attacks are the same. Some assaults develop and escalate over time. The greater the time span preceding a violent encounter, the greater your opportunity will be to access improvised weapons near you. Time is your friend because it may allow you to operate with a higher state of awareness as it relates to your environment. This higher state of readiness should permit you to more quickly identify a tool in the environment, acquire it, and use it against the threat you're defending against.

In an ambush-type attack, it's obvious that the lack of time available will reduce your opportunity to see and acquire objects in the zone of danger. That fact suggests that you should possess tools that will help you in a violent confrontation before the confrontation. Be ready in advance of the threat to use legal objects to defend yourself. Especially while under stress of a violent attack, it's much more efficient and practical to use something that's already in your possession, rather than have to identify and move toward an object located somewhere else in your surroundings. Remember, however, that even if you possess a defensive tool, you have to be ready and able to access it and properly use it to be effective.

Common Objects as Shields

Shields are common objects that you can use to block and defeat attacks directed at you and to increase the distance between you and your attacker. Shields can be used to defend against both an armed and unarmed assailant. For example, a briefcase can be used to defend against a punch, elbow strike, kick, or knee strike, as well as an attack with a stick, or against an edged weapon like a knife or a broken bottle.

Depending upon the structural integrity, composition, strength, length, and surface area of the object you use, you may be able to effectively and powerfully counterattack the assailant with it as if it were a stick. Some of the most desirable objects, such as a fire extinguisher, umbrella, or hiking stick, may possess an edged surface and may be used as a weapon to stab or slash the attacker.

In every case, it's important to not rely solely on shield-like objects and to ignore your personal weapons. It's common to combine a defense using a shield by delivering a simultaneous attack with a punch, kick, or headbutt. For example, when using a shield, you can block your assailant's strike and deliver a simultaneous kick to your opponent's groin.

If the object is large enough, it may be used to cut off the assailant from chasing you. In essence, it can serve as a barrier to separate you from your attacker. An example of this is to overturn a chair or table in the path of the aggressor.

Be aware that some common objects may not have the structural integrity (e.g., they lack a hard surface) to effectively strike or stab the assailant. If the object is heavy or bulky, its shape or size may prevent you from striking with it. In these cases, once the initial defenses are made, as demonstrated in the following section, the shield can be abandoned when safe to do so in favor of using your personal weapons or to escape from the scene.

Examples of common objects as shields:

- Laptop computer
- Backpack
- Book
- Briefcase
- Purse
- Chair
- Garbage can lid
- Plates/pots
- Lids to a pot
- Towels
- Clothing
- Walking stick

Defenses Using Two Hands on the Defensive Weapon

Defending with both hands on the defensive shield-like weapon is a very strong and natural method of defending. This method also offers the defender a great measure of control and accuracy. However, it tends to be a bit slower and the range of the defense or your reach is not as great as with a single-hand grip on a shield-like object.

Blocking Attacks at a 90° Angle

The principles used here should be familiar to you because these defenses are conceptually very similar to the 360° Defense drills (page 84). Since the defenses are designed to cover the body 360° from outside attacks, some of the defenses may overlap. In some cases, the choice of which defense to use will depend on the relative position between you and the attacker. When using a two-hand grip, the initial block or stop should be perpendicular to the attack to absorb the impact and to directly stop the force of the attack.

1 Ideally, your hands should hold the defensive object very close to the end of the object, with your arms extended.

2 You should attempt to intercept or block the middle of the weapon at a 90° angle, thereby stopping the attack. Make a body defense to be certain that you're in the safety zone created by the object, shielding you from being hit.

3 Then counterattack with the object you possess. Use the common object, along with your personal weapons, to strike and disable the assailant and end the threat to your safety.

Some examples of using common objects as shields

Redirecting/Deflecting an Attack

A common object can effectively redirect (as opposed to stop) both unarmed attacks (such as a series of punches and kicks) and armed attacks involving edged weapons (such as a knife) or blunt objects (such as a stick). The goal is for the defender to avoid being hit or stabbed by deflecting the attack. This redirection option is preferable, especially when the common object is not as strong as the weapon used in the attack.

A good illustration of this scenario is using a rolled-up magazine to deflect a straight punch or downward stab. The magazine is not strong enough to stop the attack, but it can deflect the line of the attack. After using the common object to deflect an attack, you should use it to unleash powerful and disabling counterattacks to the assailant. Of course, it's not possible in this book to include all angles of attack, positional considerations, states of readiness, and other variables. The purpose of the section is to introduce readers to the basic techniques, tactics, and principles.

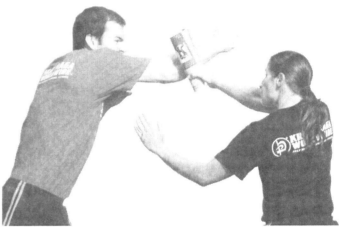

Blocking attacks at 90° angle

Common Objects as Impact Weapons

Improvised impact weapons can be sticks, umbrellas, heavy flashlights, and other objects that enable you to strike or thrust a stab at an attacker from an appropriate safe distance. An impact weapon can be used to defeat an impending attack by striking the assailant from a safe distance before he closes in to assault you. In a scenario where the assailant reaches out to catch, punch, or kick you, use the reach advantage of the object to defend by striking his hands, wrists, and virtually any bony part of his limbs or forearms.

Examples of common objects as blunt striking weapons:

- Books
- Broom
- Hammer
- Shoe
- Water bottle (filled)

- Baseball bat
- Chair
- Heavy ashtray
- Umbrella

- Mop
- Flashlight
- Rock/brick
- Telephone/cell phone

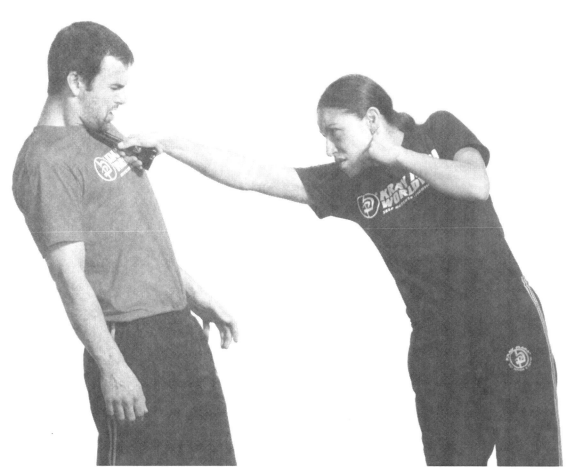

Common Objects as Chain-like Weapons

Common objects such as belts, rubber hoses, leashes, ropes, and cables can be used to injure and distract your adversary by whipping, choking, or garroting him. The approach is simple: Attack with a whipping motion by swinging to the attacker's head, face, eyes, throat, neck, torso, etc. The primary goal is to distract the attacker and to seize that opportunity to aggressively attack or to flee the zone of danger.

Examples of common objects as chain-like weapons:

- Rope
- Belt
- Chain
- Hose
- Cable
- Tree branch
- Wire
- Phone cord
- Electrical cord
- Dog leash
- Pet collar
- Bicycle lock and cable

Common Objects as Edged Weapons

Objects in the class of edged weapons have common attributes in that they're sharp and/or formed to a distinct point. When slashing or stabbing with these objects, all of the force delivered is transferred and impacts the target in a relatively small surface area. This causes maximum penetration on the targeted area of the assailant's body so that the force delivered inflicts slash- and puncture-type wounds. These injuries can immediately disable and stop the assailant. An attacker can be disabled or suffer a fatal wound when vital organs are penetrated and/or major blood vessels are severed. Objects such as a knife, a screwdriver, or even a pen can pierce the eye, neck, throat, windpipe, or torso. Remember, this is appropriate in a "kill or be killed" scenario. See the "Use of Force" section on page 15 to understand the use of force laws that govern your conduct during a fight for your life.

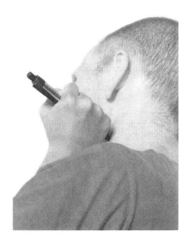

Examples of common objects as edged/cutting weapons:

- Knife
- Keys
- Pen/pencil
- Scissors
- Razor
- Box cutter
- Screwdriver
- Broken eyeglasses
- Broken glass or bottle
- Broken mirror
- Broken comb/brush

Common Objects to Distract or Blind

Various common objects and items can be used to distract or temporarily blind an assailant. These include an object or liquid item that can be suddenly thrown or sprayed at an attacker's face, which is likely to divert his attention so that you can deliver a series of attacks to vulnerable areas of his body, and/or give you the time and opportunity to escape from the zone of danger.

Examples of common objects used to distract or blind:

- Fire
- Coins
- Saliva
- Aerosols
- Dirt/sand
- Ashes from an ashtray
- Melted wax
- Sprays
- Liquids
- Hot/cold beverages

Dealing with Multiple Attackers

While confronting one attacker is very difficult, confronting multiple attackers can seem impossible. However, in a multiple attacker situation, the "rules" and/or principles of "the fight" do not change much. The key is to only engage one at a time. In other words, make it a single-attacker situation, with as many attackers as you have.

Movement

When confronted with more than one attacker, movement becomes extremely important. You should do everything possible to move in a way that "lines up" your attackers, allowing only one at a time to be in range to touch you (and you to touch them).

Lining up your attackers will also serve to confound them, making the one in front question where his partner(s) is and the partner(s) to become frustrated with being unable to engage. Generally, it's best to use upper body combatives since you can continue to move more readily. Kicks and knees force you to stop and compromise your balance. Your combatives should be powerful and your attacks visceral. This is even more important here since you'll transition from one attacker to another until you're able to escape—you don't want previous attackers rejoining the fight. It's also recommended that you don't go between attackers whenever possible. The following positioning drill is a great way to learn to line up attackers and continue to move while avoiding going between attackers. This positioning drill may be performed with three participants, but it's most effective with four or more.

1 You (the defender) are in the middle. The others begin walking toward you with their arms out (picture the classic zombie walk.)

2-3 Redirect the attackers at the arms, maintaining a safe position to the outside of the attackers. Begin adding other participants, until you're using each person as an obstacle, redirecting them into the others. Emphasize staying to the outside of the attackers and avoiding going between attackers.

DEALING WITH MULTIPLE ATTACKERS **175**

Dealing with a hostile crowd

Crowds

In some situations, you'll be unable to maneuver around a crowd, forcing you to go "through" them. There are two primary responses here, based on the "type" of crowd.

Hostile Crowd

When the crowd itself is a threat, the defender makes no allowance for the safety of those surrounding her. In this case, you should burst between attackers, preferably at the "softest" (least fortified or populated) spot while bringing your arms up, your elbows out, and keeping your head down, limiting your chances of injury. Continue to flee or search the environment for weapons, shields, or barriers. Engage only if immediate escape is not possible.

Bystander Crowd

It's possible that you'll need to navigate a crowd that's made up of bystanders, or mostly bystanders, who are not a direct threat to you. In this case, it's advisable to maneuver through the crowd as quickly as possible without harming those around you. Turn or blade your body and raise your bent lead arm in front of you to go between those around you, making as little contact as possible (think in terms of the path of least resistance).

Dealing with a bystander crowd

Using Your Environment

Whenever possible, you should at the very least be aware of your surroundings, noting where potential obstacles, hazards, bystanders, etc., may be. Ideally, your awareness should allow you to use your environment to access weapons, shields, and/or barriers to aid you in the fight (see page 166 for more details on improvised weapons). It also may be tactically sound to use one of your attackers as a barrier for a brief period if you're able to properly control and move him.

Defenses against Handgun
Threats

When an assailant points a handgun at you during a violent encounter, it presents a distinctly dangerous threat to your life. If you feel that compliance will result in your safety and will lead to surviving the encounter, you should consider complying as a means of self-preservation. Clearly, no possession is worth your life. However, it's possible that you can comply with every order and still get kidnapped, raped, and/or killed. In these dire circumstances, you may need the skills to effectively defend against an armed assailant who poses an imminent threat to your life and well-being.

It's important to know that most crimes involving a gun take place within three to five feet of the defender. Gunmen generally come close to terrorize, control, and intimidate. They also operate in this manner to hide their actions from bystanders. You can operate to defend yourself if the gun is held within or just beyond your immediate reach. While five feet is an extreme range for gun defenses, the possibility for taking effective defensive measures, even at this distance, exists.

The key principle in the Krav Maga defenses against handgun threats is this: ONCE YOU HAVE REDIRECTED THE LINE OF FIRE, DO NOT GO BACK INTO THE LINE OF FIRE AND DO NOT PERMIT THE LINE OF FIRE TO BE REDIRECTED AT YOU. Every technique strictly adheres to this basic principle.

Having a handgun pointed directly at you is an extraordinary and traumatic event. As with all Krav Maga techniques, these defenses must work under stress. The gun defenses are also designed to work when the assailant presents the gun in a variety of different positions. Utilizing the smallest number of defensive techniques to work against the largest number of variations of threats made with a gun is a key component to making the defender as safe as possible.

This section deals with extreme, high-risk scenarios in which an assailant, armed with a handgun, poses an imminent threat to your life. These extreme scenarios are common in violent crimes committed against women and may include threats from all possible angles; however, this book shall address the following common scenarios: (1) from in front of the defender (chest and head levels); (2) to the rear of the defender; and (3) to the side of the defender, behind the arm. All attacks involving a threat with a handgun are brutally stressful and highly dangerous to life and limb.

In the situations presented here, the assailant is within two to five feet (or even less) of the defender, choosing a close proximity to intimidate the defender and disguise his intentions from other parties. In defending against a gun threat, you'll only be able to defend when the gun is within your reach or slightly beyond it.

Handguns, when carried by criminals, are often used to intimidate, threaten, move, take property, or kill. An assailant using a handgun typically derives "power" from the weapon. This is significant, since once a defense is made, the assailant loses his "power" and he, too, will be in a life-or-death struggle. Expect the assailant to be fighting for his life.

Action-Reaction

Gun threats are not made in a vacuum. A gunman who sticks a gun in your face wants something. It may be your possessions, the satisfaction of humiliating you, or the thrill of terrorizing and controlling another human being. Whatever the particular motivation, the gunman who threatens you generally does so to elicit some desired result, not simply to execute you early in the confrontation. This fact affords us the opportunity to make a defense.

If you ask people what component the defender is "racing" against when trying to make a defense before the gunmen fires his weapon, most people will answer, "The act of the gunman pulling the trigger." This is entirely incorrect. The defender is not racing against an assailant's ability to merely pull the trigger. If that were true, every gun defense would fail.

The defender is, in fact, racing against the gunman's perception of any efforts to defend and the time it takes for him to make a decision that he should pull the trigger, plus the delay in real time that it takes to commence performing the physical act of pulling the trigger. Therefore, gun defenses, especially the initial redirection, must involve the least detectable motions possible. This adversely affects the gunman's perception and decision-making process, and thereby considerably slows down his ability to pull the trigger.

The Krav Maga system of gun defenses is purposely designed to have a relatively small number of distinct principles, yet offer defenses against virtually every common gun threat. We want the defender to be able to successfully operate against the largest number of gun threats using the fewest number of defensive movements.

Be aware, however: The more complex a defense system and the more decisions a defender has to make before engaging the threat, the more likely the defender will fail under the stress of a real-life confrontation involving a handgun. At the moment an assailant approaches you with a firearm, feelings of fear and intimidation and the resulting stress may interfere with your ability to react physically and psychologically to the danger. This becomes overwhelming if you have to think through and then respond by performing complex, intricate movements.

Krav Maga builds one to react in a minimal amount of time while under extreme emotional and physical stress. The Krav Maga principles and training drills that apply to addressing unarmed threats and attacks also apply to more serious threats involving weapons, like handguns. The general approach for both unarmed and armed attacks is concise, intuitive, and simple to perform. This carefully conceived design works to increase the defender's ability to react correctly and without hesitation to a threat with a handgun.

This sound and simple approach is the reason why Krav Maga works well for law-enforcement and military personnel. The needs of sworn personnel require defenses to be performed under stressful, real-life conditions. Krav Maga handgun defenses have worked to defeat deadly threats directed at on-duty peace officers and military operators. They credit their success in the field to Krav Maga's simple, easy-to-perform techniques. Ease of use and simple and direct tactics serve to prevent failing or freezing in the face of danger. This concept works for law enforcement and the military, and it'll work to improve your level of safety as well.

Important Note: NEVER train with a live (real) handgun, even if it's unloaded.

Important Considerations

When dealing with gun threats, there are many factors that go into establishing the best course of action. In order to do this in "real" time, while under stress, you should commit to memory a few tangible (though not concrete) reference points that may serve to improve your defense by increasing your speed in the defense and by reducing the ability for the assailant to pull the trigger while you're in the line of fire.

In the following defenses, references will be made to "centerline," "live" side, "dead" side, "short" side, and "long" side.

Handgun Overview

Handguns, which come in many shapes, sizes, and types, appear in all scenarios presented here. For this book, there's some value in making a distinction between a semiautomatic handgun and a revolver. While revolvers still outnumber semiautomatics in the U.S., those numbers are narrowing.

It's recommended that if you're training to defend against handgun threats, you should have at least a cursory knowledge of the different types of handguns and how they work. A *semiautomatic* has a "slide" on the top of the gun that loads a live cartridge (bullet) into the chamber in preparation for the next shot. When held, the slide will not function properly, thereby likely preventing a new round from being loaded and perhaps causing the weapon to malfunction. This is significant if the defender, once making the takeaway , chooses to fire the gun at the assailant in reasonable self-defense. To do so, it'll be necessary to "tap and rack," or load another round by clearing the chamber. Note: If there's already a round in the chamber, holding the slide will NOT affect that round or prevent it from firing.

A *revolver* has a cylinder, instead of a slide, that rotates to allow the next "live" round to move into proper position below the hammer or firing pin in order to be fired. If the revolver is in single-action mode, meaning the hammer of the weapon is already cocked, and the defender grabs the cylinder, this will NOT prevent the revolver from firing the first round, nor will this cause a malfunction in the revolver. However, if the defender grabs and holds the cylinder, it will not turn, which prevents a new round from being loaded into a position to be fired.

Centerline   *Live side*   *Dead side*

Centerline: the relative center of the defender's body in its profile to the line of fire

Live side: the side of the defender's body where attacks by the assailant are most readily available (generally thought of as inside the elbows or the front of the body)

Dead side: the side of the defender's body where attacks by the assailant are least readily available (generally thought of as outside the elbows or the back of the body)

Short side: the proximity of the line of fire in relation to the centerline of the defender and the area of the body with the shortest line off the body

Long side: the proximity of the line of fire in relation to the centerline of the defender and the area of the body with the longest line off the body

Centerline   *Short side*   *Long side*

DEFENSES AGAINST HANDGUN THREATS **181**

After a disarm is made, the defender has several "after action" options available. Some of these are:

- Tapping and racking the weapon (make it ready to fire)
- Keeping the assailant in the line of fire, but keeping the weapon at a safe distance to avoid the assailant from reacquiring the gun
- Using the weapon dry (i.e., striking with it)
- Using personal weapons/combatives
- Accessing own weapons

Regardless of which action you choose, all should serve to put you in a safer position.

Important *Safety in Training* Note: Do NOT put your finger on the trigger and do not place the trigger finger along the frame of the gun when training on any of the handgun defenses as it may get broken.

Threat

THREAT The assailant presents the handgun at your centerline. In this case, it's at your chest or abdomen, although it could be at your head (see variation).

DANGER You may be shot or taken to another location, where further crimes will be committed.

SOLUTION

1 As the gun is presented, send your left hand to the weapon in a straight line, putting the side of your index finger at the side of the weapon. Move the weapon in a straight line to your right. The movement should take the gun off your body parallel to the floor. Just as your hand reaches the weapon and begins to redirect it, make a body defense by allowing your left shoulder to come forward, blading your body. This has the added benefit of putting your motion and weight toward the gunman even though your feet have not yet moved. Any diagonal movement up or down means that the line of fire will stay on your body for a longer period of time. Also, note that this movement takes the weapon from vital areas (center of the chest) to areas that are less and less vital, until the gun is completely off. IN ADDITION, THIS INITIAL REDIRECTION MUST INVOLVE NO OTHER BODY MOVEMENT: NO LEANING, NO TENSING, NO SHIFT OF YOUR FEET, NO UNNECESSARY FACIAL EXPRESSIONS. The gun need only be redirected to the outside until it's in front of your opposite hip.

continued on next page

DEFENSES AGAINST HANDGUN THREATS **183**

continued from previous page

2 Grab the weapon sharply and "punch" it down so that the gun points 90° away from you and is roughly parallel with the floor. You should already be putting weight down on the weapon. As you redirect, your right hand can already be coming up to punch, but it should be close to your body so that it isn't in the line of fire.

3 As you burst in, keep your weight on the weapon by "punching" it down toward the attacker's midsection—deliver a punch to the face or throat with your right hand. Always make sure your weight stays on the weapon!

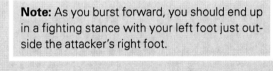

Note: As you burst forward, you should end up in a fighting stance with your left foot just outside the attacker's right foot.

4 Recoil your punch.

5-6 Slide your hand along your body to avoid the line of fire. Reach down and grab the weapon at the hammer.

7 Rotate the gun sharply 45° to "break" it from the gunman's grasp. Note that this may break the gunman's finger. In training, DO NOT allow the "attacker" to put their finger in the trigger guard or to index it along the frame of the gun.

continued on next page

continued from previous page

8 As soon as the weapon has rotated to loosen the attacker's grip, pull it toward your rear hip. Note that your feet haven't moved yet!

9 As soon as you're sure the weapon is in your possession, retreat to a safe distance.

To the Head Variation: This technique is the same as the regular Defense against Threat with a Handgun from the Front, with one difference. Since the threat is to the head versus the body, a head movement is necessary to get out of the line of fire. You make an earlier body defense by moving your head even before your hand has reached the gun (although the hand always leads the motion). This is possible because the movement to get you out of the line of fire is shorter and simpler than moving your whole body.

Threat

THREAT The assailant presents the handgun to the back of the defender, with the weapon touching. In this case, it's at the defender's lower back, although it could be higher on the back or at the back of the head. The line of fire is directed to the centerline of the defender's back or toward the defender's right, which dictates redirecting the line of fire in that direction.

DANGER The defender may be shot in the place where she's first attacked or be escorted/taken to another location, where further crimes will be committed.

SOLUTION

1 As the gun is pressed to your back, look behind you. You aren't really concerned about what's touching your body. You need to make sure a gun isn't in the assailant's other ("off") hand. Leading with your arm, turn or roll in deeply enough to redirect the weapon and take your body out of the line of fire. Note that if the gun is held low, your arm will make the redirection along with the body defense. However, if the gun is held high on your back, the arm will have little or no effect, and you'll create a defense by sharply turning or rolling in along the assailant's arm. However, the arm still helps your body rotate.

continued on next page

DEFENSES AGAINST HANDGUN THREATS **187**

continued from previous page

2–5 While bursting in, reach with your left hand deep under the assailant's arm. Your left foot should be to the outside and deeper than the assailant's right foot. Bring your left arm up, trapping the weapon arm against your body while sliding your left arm back to the wrist of the weapon hand. This control works on the handcuff principle and is very strong. Your controlling hand should be in a fist, and your arm should be pinned very tightly to your body. Strike the assailant's face or throat with your right elbow as soon as possible in relation to rolling in to perform the body defense. The momentum generated when striking at the same time you move in adds considerable power to your elbow strike. Once you've established control of the weapon arm, you may send additional counterattacks with knees and/or kicks to the groin (additional upper body combatives are also possible). (Images 3–8 show the reverse view.)

6–7 Bringing your left shoulder up and slightly forward, reach over with your right hand, pinky side up, and grab the end of the barrel of the weapon. *Note:* Keep your eyes on the assailant and be sure not to turn your back to him.

8 To break the grip, snap the muzzle of the weapon down or flat toward the ground but not enough to allow the line of fire to be placed on your body, bringing your entire arm down.

continued on next page

DEFENSES AGAINST HANDGUN THREATS

continued from previous page

9 Lift the weapon straight up for the takeaway.

10–11 Deliver counterattacks, such as elbows and weapon strikes, and get out without tripping and move to a safe distance away from the assailant.

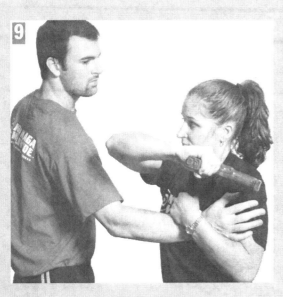

Additional Notes: Be sure your hold on the wrist is strong. Press your fist to your chest. Push your shoulder forward. Note that this is your shoulder, not your whole upper body

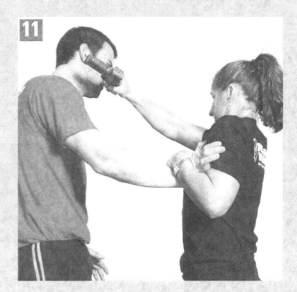

Gun to the Side of the Body behind the Arm Variation: The defense in this threat scenario is virtually the same as when the gun is placed to your back. However, in this case, the gun is touching your side and is placed behind your arm. To defend, make a small redirection with your arm, pushing the gun and the line of fire behind you. This movement should be relatively small. Otherwise, the defense is exactly the same as Threat with a Handgun from Behind—Touching.

HELPFUL HINTS

- As you redirect the weapon, the gunman will probably pull the weapon back. If you don't burst in, you'll be in the line of fire. Bursting in ensures that you'll get deep enough to keep control of the weapon.
- In general, you can't give a punch instead of an elbow—not because of the elbow itself, but because giving an elbow forces you to get in deep where you can more easily control the weapon. A punch is possible for people much shorter than the attacker. However, always be sure you're getting in deep.
- It's extremely important to make the "handcuff" technique because this controls the weapon as the gunman struggles. Also, if he falls because of the elbow strike, this hold ensures that you won't lose the gun.
- Defenders often "wind up" their arm before making the redirection. This is unnecessary as the defensive movement to redirect can be very small.

Defenses against
Edged-Weapon Threats

This section covers practical and proven techniques to effectively deal with an assailant who uses an edged weapon to pose an imminent threat to the life of the defender. An edged weapon, while typically a knife, could be any short instrument used to cut or stab, such as a broken bottle, scissors, box cutter, screwdriver, etc.

There are several key factors that should be considered when dealing with a threat (as opposed to an attack). The behavior of the assailant is different from one who is actively stabbing or slashing at the defender. The assailant may want to gain information or property from the victim, take the victim hostage and/or move the victim to another location. Depending on the nature and context of the threat, a knife-wielding assailant has the ability to threaten the intended victim from close, intermediate, and long-range distances, at various angles and heights, and by placing the edged weapon at different parts of the victim's body.

> **Note:** Generally, the defender's hands are down by the sides. Bringing the hands up and then making a defense is a "bigger" movement that's much more obvious to the assailant. If the assailant orders the defender's hands up, this is an ideal time to make the defense (if in range) since the assailant expects movement.

Our experiences have taught us that each passing second may allow the situation to escalate into a more dangerous and dynamic scenario, one in which the assailant actively attacks with the edged weapon by stabbing and slashing repeatedly at the intended victim. Just like in basic handgun techniques, the technical principles for addressing knife threats are Redirect, Control, Attack, and Take Away. The tactical responses generally recommended are: (1) escape; (2) use an improvised weapon or shield; and/or (3) unarmed defense coupled with a highly aggressive counterattack on the assailant using your personal weapons.

This section will address the least desirable but most problematic response—the use of personal weapons. In the cases presented here, the defender has no method of escape or weapons/shields of expedience. It's important to note that once an initial defense is made, there are four common responses from the assailant: switch knife hands, thrust the knife forward, pull the knife away, and/or strike. The techniques described here are designed to address all of these concerns. Furthermore, this section will address defensive principles that apply to threats with an edged weapon to the front of the defender and to the rear of the defender. Unique defensive techniques and tactics, and how to perform them under varying degrees of stress, will also be covered.

> **Basic Knife-Threat Defense Principles**
>
> **Redirect:** Move the edge away from your body.
>
> **Control:** Get control of the weapon hand.
>
> **Attack:** Send aggressive counterattacks to the assailant.
>
> **Take Away:** Disarm the assailant.

The Weapon

An edged weapon may be a carefully crafted, dedicated weapon, such as a knife carried on one's person, or a weapon of convenience, such as scissors or a broken bottle. While the actual attack range is limited, the edged weapon presents multiple problems for defenders.

Edged weapons are easily concealed and, quite often, victims are unaware of the presence of a knife. Edged weapons are typically easy to wield and difficult to isolate for the defender. Such weapons are always "live," never run out of "ammo," and almost never fail. For these reasons, among others, edged weapons are often considered the hardest to deal with. In addition, according to police reports submitted annually to the FBI, a person in the U.S. who is stabbed by a knife is 20 percent more likely to die than one who suffers a gun shot.

The Assailant

A person willing to use such a weapon is characteristically of a different mindset from one preferring other, longer-range weapons. An assailant choosing to brandish and use an edged weapon is willing to go "hands on"—to get bloody, to feel metal against bone and tendon, and to feel the life leave the victim. A person with this capacity must be met with equal or greater ferocity if the defender is to have a chance of survival.

Edged-Weapon Threats from the Front

In all of the scenarios given, assume the knife is being held in the right hand. The emphasis is almost always on controlling the weapon and counterattacking aggressively. While disarms are shown, the "real" defense is in the offense. Counterattacks should be of a nature that renders the assailant unable or unwilling to continue the attack.

Edged Weapon Touching or at Short Distance off the Body

Threat

THREAT The attacker is close to you and presents the knife to the front of your body. The knife may be touching you or simply held close to your body. The knife is not necessarily held statically—the assailant may be moving it around, giving directions, pointing, threatening, etc. The assailant may wish to move you to another location.

SOLUTION

1 With your left hand, grab the assailant's weapon-hand wrist, redirecting the weapon toward your right side. Because of the proximity of the threat, you should attempt to control the weapon in the assailant's hand and counterattack aggressively.

2 As soon as possible, reach your right hand to control the weapon hand, covering the hand as much as possible. Extend your arms away from you, applying weight and creating distance. Tuck your chin behind your right shoulder to minimize the chance of being struck in the face.

3–4 As soon as your right hand has contact with the attacker's fist, bring the attacker's wrist up above or over his elbow. Apply downward pressure to the hand while pulling slightly with your left hand, which is on his wrist. At about the same time, send a front kick to the groin. Don't wait for one to do the other—the control and counter could be performed nearly at the same time.

5 Maintain control at the wrist using your whole body, with the palm of your right hand applying pressure to the knuckles of the assailant's weapon hand. The pressure should force the fingers surrounding the knife to open. While maintaining contact, scrape the weapon out of the assailant's hand.

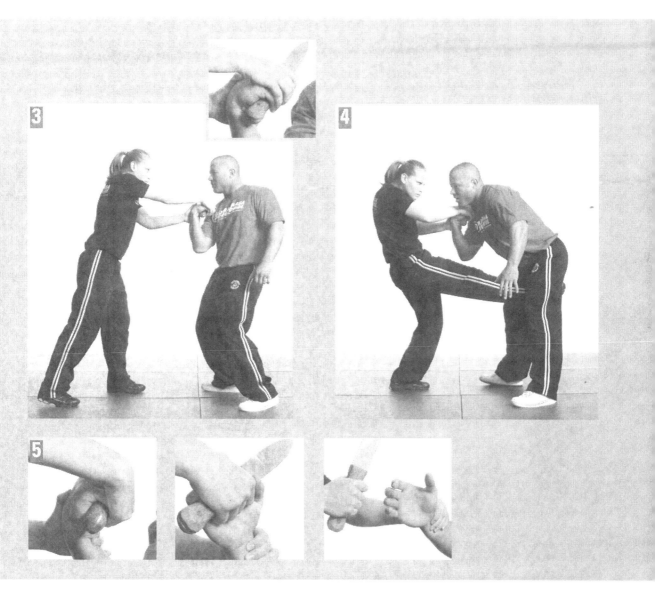

Threat

THREAT The attacker stands farther away from you and presents the knife to the front of your body. The threat may be the same as with the knife closer to the body but, because of the distance, getting your second hand to secure the assailant's knife hand quickly is difficult or implausible. The knife is not necessarily held statically—the assailant may be moving it around, giving directions, pointing, threatening, etc.

SOLUTION

1 Using the palm of your left hand, redirect the weapon hand toward your right and slightly up with a quick and explosive striking movement to the back of the assailant's hand. *Note:* Redirecting slightly upward yields less resistance from the assailant. Also, your left shoulder should move forward, which angles the body and increases your reach.

2 Immediately, after redirecting the weapon hand, burst diagonally forward to the dead side of the assailant, leaning your upper body back and sending a powerful front kick to the groin. Be sure to move at an angle that's in the opposite direction of the redirected weapon hand. Immediately seek to escape or acquire an object that may be used as a shield or weapon.

Edged-Weapon Threats from Behind

In all of the scenarios given, assume the knife is being held in the right hand. The emphasis is almost always on controlling the weapon and counterattacking aggressively. While disarms are shown, the "real" defense is in the offense. Counterattacks should be of a nature that renders the assailant unable or unwilling to continue the attack.

Edged Weapon at Back, Touching

Threat

THREAT The attacker touches the knife to your back. While the assailant's intent may be to move you or take property, you're very vulnerable to stabs to the back. When responding to this threat, it's important to take a quick look over or around your shoulder to determine that the weapon (not the assailant's hand or fingers) is actually at your back and not held in his off or back hand. Krav Maga practitioners familiar with basic handgun defenses will find the response to this threat very similar.

SOLUTION

1–2 After determining that the weapon is indeed placed at your back, turn toward the left, with your left arm leading the motion. As your left arm redirects the weapon, continue to reach with your left arm extended forward and burst in very deep, reaching your left arm toward the assailant's underarm.

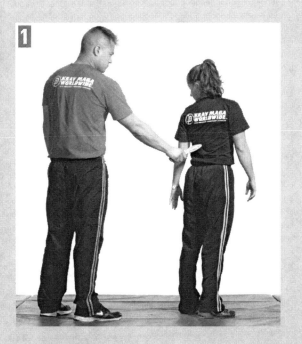

continued on next page

DEFENSES AGAINST EDGED-WEAPON THREATS **197**

continued from previous page

3 Once inside, wrap your left arm up and around, trapping the assailant's arm to your body. Your left arm should slide to the assailant's wrist while delivering an elbow to the assailant's face with your right arm. Follow up with additional counterattacks, including knees, kicks, etc.

4 Maintaining control and leverage on the assailant's wrist, reach over with your right hand and cover the weapon hand.

5-7 While applying pressure to the assailant's wrist and shoulder, rotate the weapon hand so that his palm faces up and his fingers are forced open. Without losing contact or control, scrape the knife out of the assailant's hand.

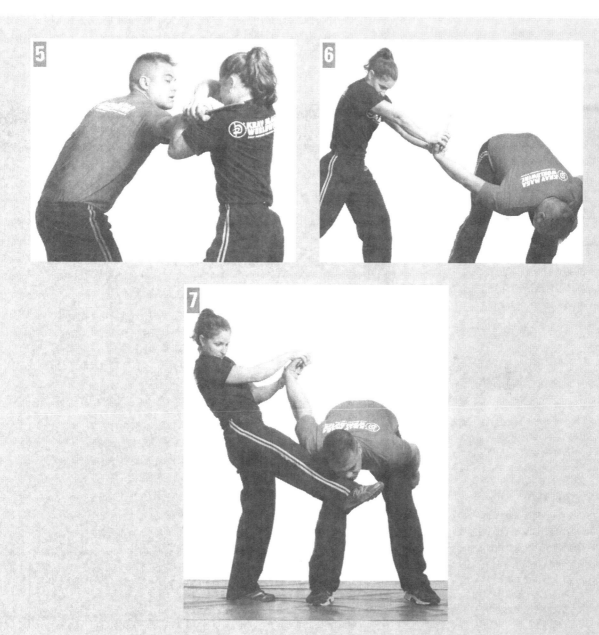

A

Aggressiveness drills, 14
Arm Pull from Behind, 126
Arm Pull from the Front or Side, 125
Attackers, multiple, 174–77
Awareness drills, 14
Awareness skills, 23–24

B

Back Kick, 73–74
Bearhug from Behind with Arms
    Caught, 142–43
Bearhug from Behind with Arms Free,
    144–45
Bearhug from Behind with Arms Free
    (Variation #1), 146–48
Bearhug from Behind with Lift, 149
Bearhug from the Front with Arms
    Caught, 135
Bearhug from the Front with Arms
    Free (Basic), 136
Bearhug from the Front with Arms
    Free (Variation #1), 137–38
Bearhug from the Front with Arms
    Free (Variation #2), 139
Bearhug from the Front with Lift,
    140–41

Bearhugs, defenses against, 134–49
Biting, 44
Blinding weapons, 173
Body language, 21, 24, 27, 28
Both Wrists Grabbed, Held Behind the
    Back, 123–24
Both Wrists Grabbed, High, 121–22
Both Wrists Grabbed, Low, 120
Boundaries, 24–26

C

Castle Doctrine, 17
Chain-like weapons, 172
Choke from Behind (in Place), 97–98
Choke from Behind with Push
    Forward, 102–104
Choke from the Front (in Place),
    93–94
Choke from the Front with Push
    Backward, 99–101
Choke from the Side (in Place), 95–96
Chokes, 93–104
Color Code System of Awareness,
    23
Cross-Side Grab, 115–16
Crowds, 176–77

D

De-escalation tactics, 28–29
Defending Strikes while Mounted,
    152–53
Defense against Threat with a
    Handgun from Behind—Touching,
    187–91
Defense against Threat with a
    Handgun from the Front, 183–86
Defenses against bearhugs, 134–49
Defenses against unarmed attacks,
    83, 149
Defenses against wrist grabs and arm
    pulls, 111–26
Defensive Front Kick, 68
Defensive weapons, 166–73
Distraction weapons, 173
Downward Stomping Kick, 76
Drills, 12–14

E

Edged Weapon at Back, Touching,
    197–99
Edged Weapon at Longer Distance off
    the Body, 196
Edged Weapon Touching or at Short
    Distance off the Body, 194–95

Edged weapons: defenses against, 192–99; defensive, 172–73
Elbow strikes, 53–60
Environment awareness, 23–24
Equipment, 38–39
Escaping Mount: Elbow Escape, 157–58
Escaping Mount: Trap and Roll, 154–56
Escaping Mount and Two–Hand Choke, 159–60
Escaping the Guard (and Getting Back to Your Feet), 161–62
Eye contact, 27

F

Facial expressions, 27
Fatigue drills, 14
Fighting stance, 41
Fist, making, 45
Fist punches, 45–47
Focus mitts, 39
Force, defined, 15; use of, 10, 15–19
Forearm Strike, 61
Front Kick from the Ground, 78

G

Gloves, 39
Gouging, 44
Grabbing, 44
Groundfighting, 150–65
Guns, defenses against, 178–91

H

Hair Grab from the Front (Static), 129–30
Hair Grab from the Front or Side (Impending Knee Strike), 132
Hair Grab from the Opposite Side or Back of the Head, 133
Hair Grab from the Side with Pull, 131
Hammerfist Punch Downward, 51
Hammerfist Punch to the Front, 50

Hammerfist Punch to the Side or Back, 52
Hammerfist punches, 49–52
Handguns, defenses against, 178–91
Handwraps, 39
Headbutt, 62
Headlock from Behind, 108–10
Headlock from the Side, 105–107
Headlocks, 105–10
Heel Punch, 48
Horizontal Plane: Elbow #1, 54
Horizontal Plane: Elbow #2, 55
Horizontal Plane: Elbow #3, 56
Hostage Position from Behind, 127–28

I

Impact weapons, 171
Inside Defense against Punches and Other Strikes, 90–91
Inside Defense and 360° Defense Drill against Punches, 92
"Interview process," 21
Intuition, 23

K

Kicking from Guard and Getting Up, 163–65
Kicks, 63–81; from a lying position, 77–81
Kickshield pads, 38
Knee Strike, 64
Knives, defenses against, 192–99
Krav Maga: characteristics, 8–10; equipment, 38–39; history, 7; techniques, 8, 37–199; training, 8, 11–14, 37–39, 40–44; use of force issues, 10, 15–19
Krav Maga Worldwide, 9

L

Legal issues, 15–19
Leverage on joints, 44

M

Making a Fist, 45
Mouthpieces, 39

N

National Sexual Assault Hotline, 32, 34
Neutral position, 41

O

Objects, common, as defensive weapons, 166–73
Offensive Front Kick, 67

P

Pads, 38
Peripheral vision, 23–24
Personal weapons, 43–44
Position of disadvantage, and training, 11–12
Punch pads, 38
Punches, 45–52

Q

Quitting, 10

R

Rape. See Sexual assault
"Reasonable person" standard, 15
Revolvers, 180
Rising Front Kick to the Groin, 66
Rising Front Kick to Upper Body, 65
Round Kick, 69–70
Round Kick from the Ground, 79–80

S

Safety, 8, 38
Same-Side Grab (Attacker's Thumb Down), 114
Same-Side Grab (Attacker's Thumb Up), 112–13
Scenario replication, and training, 12

Self-defense: "golden rules," 17–18; legal issues, 16–19
Semiautomatic guns, 180
Sexual assault: defenses against, 20–31; guidelines for victims, 34; reporting, 32–34
Shields, 168
Short Uppercut Back Kick, 75
Side Kick, 71–72
Side Kick from the Ground, 81
Straight Punch, 46
Straight Punch Low, 47
Straight punches, 45–48
Stress drills, 14
Striking surfaces, 43
Surroundings, unfamiliar, and training, 12
Survival mindset concept, 21–31

T

Tactical tips, 29–31
Target areas, 9, 42
Tearing, 44
Techniques, 8, 37–199
360° Defense Exercise, 84–88
360° Defense with Counterattack, 89
TIV concept, 27
Tombstone pads, 38
Training: 8, 11–14; 40–49; drills, 12–14; equipment, 38–39; partners, 12; positions, 40–42; preparation, 37–39; safety, 38
Two-on-One Grab, 117–19

U

Use of force issues, 10, 15–19; reporting guidelines, 18–19

V

Verbalization, 26–28
Vertical Plane: Elbow #4, 57
Vertical Plane: Elbow #5, 58
Vertical Plane: Elbow #6, 59
Vertical Plane: Elbow #7, 60
Voice. *See* Verbalization

W

Warrior mindset. *See* Survival mindset concept
Weapons, defensive, 166–73; personal, 43. *See also* Handguns; Knives

Acknowledgments

Darren Levine expresses everlasting appreciation to Imi for teaching him the way of Krav Maga. He would also like to thank all of his teachers, especially Shayke Barak and Ellie Avikzar, for their instruction and support so that he may pass the system on to others.

* * *

Marni Levine, a 4th-degree black belt in Krav Maga, was the highest-ranking female instructor in the world. She was a wife, a wonderful mother, a daughter and sister, and a valiant and true friend. In addition to all that, she was devoted to Krav Maga and worked tirelessly to make it grow. Marni Levine lost her five-year battle with breast cancer at age 37.

As a memorial tribute to an extraordinary woman, Krav Maga Worldwide and STOP CANCER have created the Marni Fund, with a shared mission dedicated to developing improved treatments, new diagnostic procedures, and the ultimate goal—a cure for breast cancer. Created in memory of Marni Levine (1969–2006), the Marni Fund is currently supporting innovative breast cancer researchers at UCLA, USC, and City of Hope NCI-designated Comprehensive Cancer Centers.

Please help us fight this horrible disease. Donations can be made to The Marni Fund. For more information, please go to www.stopcancer.net/marnifund.php.

About the Authors

Darren Levine, a 6th-degree black belt in Krav Maga, founded the nonprofit Krav Maga Association of America, Inc., at the personal request of Krav Maga Grandmaster Imi Lichtenfeld. Darren serves as the chairman of the board and U.S. chief instructor of Krav Maga Worldwide. He was certified as a Krav Maga instructor in 1981 by the Israeli Ministry of Education and the Wingate Institute of Physical Education and Sport in Netanya, Israel. Darren has taught Krav Maga to thousands of civilians and local, state, and federal law-enforcement officers, as well as to military Special Operations and counterterror units on an official basis throughout the United States and abroad. In addition, he has served as a deputy district attorney for the County of Los Angeles since 1990. As a prosecutor, he was a senior member of the Crimes against Peace Officers Section (CAPOS), an elite special-trials unit tasked with the responsibility of prosecuting the most violent crimes committed against peace officers. In that position, he has prosecuted eight cases involving the murders of on-duty peace officers and was entrusted with prosecuting some of the most challenging, complex, and high-profile cases in the Los Angeles County District Attorney's Office. Currently, he serves as a supervisor in the District Attorney's Office. He has been recognized with many awards, including the Los Angeles Deputy District Attorney of the Year (2003) and the National Association of District Attorneys (corecipient) of the 2004 Heavy Hitter Award, and was named a Distinguished Alumni of Loyola Law School in 2005. Darren continues to extensively teach Krav Maga throughout the world. In his dual roles as Krav Maga chief instructor and deputy district attorney, he has dedicated his life to the safety of others.

Ryan Hoover is a civilian, law-enforcement, and military trainer of instructors in eight different countries. He holds an advanced black belt in Krav Maga and has black belts in multiple systems. He has coauthored two other books on Krav Maga, including *Krav Maga for Beginners* and *Black Belt Krav Maga*. Ryan is a certified natural trainer with Monkey Bar Gymnasium and a speed, agility, and quickness trainer. He is also the cofounder of Fit to Fight and its requisite programs SPARology, Hard Ready, Pride, and From the Ground Up. Instrumental in developing defensive tactics curricula at the state level, he owns two training centers in North Carolina and actively trains in boxing, Muay Thai, Brazilian jiu-jitsu, and more, traveling the world not only to teach but also to train and continue to grow.

Kelly Campbell, a 3rd-degree black belt in Krav Maga, is the highest-ranking female instructor in the United States. She is a senior instructor and holds two official titles at Krav Maga Worldwide: Director of Instructor Development and Training Coordinator for the Licensing Division. She is certified in a number of other specialties, including Train the Trainer, Civilian Law Enforcement Instructor, and ASST (Adrenal Stress Scenario Training). She is also a certified KM-X instructor (Krav Maga Worldwide's youth program), and is a single mother of a teenage boy. This combination of expertise and life experience makes her a highly sought-after role model for other women.

CPSIA information can be obtained at www.ICGtesting.com
Printed in the USA
LVOW09s1037220715

447023LV00005B/25/P

9 781569 759875